LIEH TZU'S
HSING SHIH SHENG

Psychotherapeutic Commentaries

Book Cover Symbolism

Turquoise Blue • Spiritual Conductivity

Copper • Seamless/Flowing/Circulating Energy

By The Author

LAO TZU'S *TAO TE CHING*
Psychotherapeutic Commentaries
A Wayfaring Counselor's Rendering
of The Tao Virtuosity Experience
[Regent Press, 2016]

CHUANG TZU'S *NEI P'IEN*
Psychotherapeutic Commentaries
A Wayfaring Counselor's Rendering
of The Seven Interior Records
[Regent Press, 2017]

LAO TZU'S *TAO TE CHING*
Soul Journeying Commentaries
A Sojourning Pilgrim's Rendering
of 81 Spirit Soul Passages
[Regent Press, 2018]

LIEH TZU'S
HSING SHIH SHENG
Psychotherapeutic Commentaries

性實生

A WAYFARING COUNSELOR'S RENDERING

OF

THE NATURE OF REAL LIVING

Raymond Bart Vespe

REGENT PRESS
Berkeley, California

Paperback
ISBN 13: 978-1-58790-415-8
ISBN 10:1-58790-415-2

E-book
ISBN 13: 978-1-58790-416-5
ISBN 10: 1-58790-416-0

Library of Congress Control Number: 2017953018

Manufactured in the United States of America

REGENT PRESS
www.regentpress.net
regentpress@mindspring.com

CONTENTS

DEDICATION

For all of my family and relatives, friends and acquaintances, teachers and students, supervisors and supervisees, trainers and trainees, therapists and patients, counselors and clients, colleagues and associates and staff members and co-workers with whom I have enjoyed the blessed gift, precious opportunity and treasured experience of loving to learn and grow and learning and growing to love. Thank you dear, sweet, beautiful and splendid human beings.

ACKNOWLEDGEMENTS

Of Thomas Cleary, Livia Kohn and Eva Wong for their commitment to, and talent for, bringing the invaluable resources of the teachings and practices of the ancient Chinese philosophical and Spiritual tradition of Taoism to us human beings in the modern West and for making available the Way and ways that inspire, encourage, support, assist, facilitate and guide our becoming more wise, true and real Souls and living more free, peaceful and joyful lives.

Once again, of my youngest daughter, Arianna Selene Lewin and son-in-law, Ashley Evan Lewin, for their ongoing support throughout the writing of, and for their continuing assistance during the word processing of, this rendition and of Mark Weiman of Regent Press for midwifing the process of developing it from manuscript, through formatting and proofing to publication.

LIEH

列

ARRANGE IN ORDER
ENUMERATE/CLASSIFY
SET OUT/LIST/FILE/RANK
SERIES/ROW/LINE
VARIOUS/EACH AND EVERY

TZU

子

BOY/SON/CHILD
PHILOSOPHER/MASTER
ANCIENT TITLE OF RESPECT[1]

LIEH TZU

THE ALIGNING/FLOWING/FOLLOWING/
ENTRAINING/MASTER/PHILOSOPHER

PROLOGUE

The following is a brief general outline of the three principal sources and some characteristics of the ancient Chinese Spiritual and philosophical tradition of Taoism.

	LAO TZU	CHUANG TZU	LIEH TZU
Life	c. 6th Century BCE Court archivist	c. 369-286 BCE Independent scholar	c. 4th Century BCE Simple hermit
Period	Spring/Autumn c. 770-476 BCE	Warring States c. 475-221 BCE	Warring States c. 475-221 BCE
Text	*The Lao Tzu*	*The Chuang Tzu*	*The Lieh Tzu*
Title	*Tao Te Ching*	*Nei P'ien*	*Hsing Shih Sheng*
Date	? 500 BCE	? 300 BCE	? 200 BCE-? 400 CE
Form	81 Verses Adages	7 Records Tales	8 Sections Narratives
Sage	Sacred/wise Sheng Jen	True/free Chen Jen	Real/actual Shih Jen
Ethos	Sagacity	Veracity	Practicality
Focus	Wise ruling	Individual freedom	Everyday matters
Ruling	Reforming	Deconstructing	Non-Involving
Living	Accord with Tao	Accord with Heaven-Earth	Accord with Destiny
Tao	Essentially beneficial	Equally integral	Naturally neutral
Tao	Way	Heaven-Earth	Reality
Te	Virtuosity	Inborn Tao-nature	Integrity
Yin/Yang Ch'i	Alternating	Transforming	Originating
Wu Wei Ch'i	Flowing	Following	Unfolding
Tzu Jan	As-itself-so	Spontaneity	Naturalness
Wan Wu	10,000 things	Completing	Actuality
Tao Jen	Wise human being	True human being	Real human being
Letting-be	Clearness	Heart-Mind fasting	Natural state
Letting-go	Emptiness	Sitting forgetting	Natural cycle
Going-with	Stillness	Origin wandering	Natural course
Being-with	Oneness	Tao residing	Natural order
Philosophy	Taoist ontology Way of being Living unity	Taoist epistemology Way of knowing Living truth	Taoist ethics Way of doing Living right

HSING

性

Nature/quality
Character
Heart at Birth

SHIH

實

Real/actual
True/genuine
Solid/substantial

SHENG

生

Life/living
Birth/bear
Grow

HSING SHIH SHENG

The Nature Of Real Living

INTRODUCTION

Authorship and Text

The texts of ancient Chinese Taoism are characteristically initially named after their purported authors, e.g., *The Lao Tzu*, *The Chuang Tzu* and *The Lieh Tzu*. However, Lieh Tzu is said to have lived in the 4th Century BCE during the Warring States period (c. 475-221 BCE) of the Eastern Chou Dynasty (c. 770-221 BCE). While many of the narratives are set during this time period and cast Lieh Tzu as a central figure, *The Lieh Tzu* text itself reportedly is a compilation made over a six hundred year period between c. 200 BCE and c. 400 CE and no part of it could have been written by Lieh Tzu himself.

As with Lao Tzu, purported author of *The Lao Tzu*, later titled *The Tao Te Ching*, a definite determintion cannot be made concerning whether Lieh Tzu is a legendary, fictional or composite characterization or a real human being. A man by the name of Lieh Tzu, also known as Lieh Yu K'ou, is said to have been born (c. 350 BCE) in the feudal state of Cheng (c. 774-500/806-375 BCE)[2] in Central China several hundred years later than Lao Tzu (c. 6th Century BCE) and is a contemporary of Chuang Tzu (c. 365-286 BCE). Little is known about his life, except that he resides in Cheng for forty years, may have moved to the feudal state of Wei (c. 1022-241 BCE), never holds a public office and lives a simple, ordinary and peaceful life as a hermit disengaged from the affairs of the world.

Chapter 32 of *The Chuang Tzu* text is titled Lieh Yu K'ou and he appears as a character in several tales of the text, e.g., as someone who variously rides the wind, meets a shaman, talks to a skull, demonstrates archery skills, attracts a following and refuses alms from a ruler. An individual named Lieh Tzu reportedly authored *The True Book of Expanding Emptiness/Ch'ung*

Hsu Chen Ching, however, sinologists date this text at c. 300 CE in the time of the Chin Dynasty (c. 265-420 CE) much later than Lieh Tzu's life.

Lieh Tzu appears throughout various narratives of *The Lieh Tzu* text, Lao Tzu[3] and Wen Tzu[4] appear in several of the narratives, Chuang Tzu[5] is mentioned once and Sections Four and Seven are respectively titled for the philosophers K'ung Fu Tzu/Confucius[6] and Yang Chu.[7] Nearly one half of the narratives in Section Two are also found in *The Chuang Tzu* text re:, e.g., an immortal, a shaman, an unteachable disciple, an archer, a ferryman, a swimmer, a cicada catcher, a tiger keeper, a rooster trainer, a monkey feeder, an innkeeper and a drunken man.

Lieh Tzu is considered, along with Lao Tzu and Chuang Tzu, to be one of the principal foundational human beings in the ancient Chinese philosophical and Spiritual tradition of Taoism. *The Lieh Tzu* text has been translated into the three English language works cited in the references of this rendition.

Titles

The original titles of each of the eight sections of *The Lieh Tzu* text generally correspond to their initial narratives and, in this rendition, are included as subtitles. The main titles of each narrative are named according to an interpretation of their central themes. The following is a listing of the titles of the eight sections of this rendition of *The Lieh Tzu* text and their respective corresponding Chinese translations; subtitles, correlated principal experiential concepts and being-states.

While the undergoing and experiencing of the wayfaring journeying of human beings are fundamentally and essentially multidimensional, simultaneous and non-linear; the eight sections of *The Lieh Tzu* text can be viewed as progressive developmental stages occurring throughout our human life course, life cycle and life span.

SECTION ONE
- ❖ The Nature of Originating/Yuan/Heaven's Bestowal.
- ❖ Ch'i/Cosmic/Vital Energy of/*as* Tao.
- ❖ Non-Being/InSpiriting/Animating/Activating/Aliveness.

SECTION TWO
- ❖ The Nature of Transcending/Ch'ao/Yellow Emperor.
- ❖ Te/Potent Virtuosity of/*as* Tao.
- ❖ Letting-Be/Individuating/Accepting/Acknowledging/ Uniqueness.

SECTION THREE
- ❖ The Nature of Transforming/Hua/King Mu.
- ❖ Yin/Yang Ch'i/Dynamic Bipolarity of/*as* Tao.
- ❖ Letting-Go/Non-Attaching/Attuning/According/ Emptiness.

SECTION FOUR
- ❖ The Nature of Awakening/Wu/Confucius.
- ❖ Wan Wu/Phenomenal Totality of/*as* Tao.
- ❖ All-Being/Illuminating/Appearing/Abounding/ Clearness.

SECTION FIVE
- ❖ The Nature of Uniting/T'ung/T'ang's Questions.
- ❖ Tao/Ultimate Reality of/*as* Tao.
- ❖ Being-With/Identifying/Affiliating/Abiding/Oneness.

SECTION SIX
- ❖ The Nature of Following/Ts'ung/Destiny.
- ❖ Wu Wei Ch'i/Kinetic Fluidity of/*as* Tao.
- ❖ Going-With/Flowing/Allowing/Accompanying/Stillness.

SECTION SEVEN
- ❖ The Nature of Enjoying/Hsiang/Yang Chu.
- ❖ Tzu Jan/Natural Spontaneity of/*as* Tao.
- ❖ This-Being/Presencing/Appreciating/Admiring/Freeness.

SECTION EIGHT

- ❖ The Nature of Completing/Ch'eng/Ch'uan/ Synchronicity.
- ❖ Tao Jen/Consummate Humanity of/*as* Tao.
- ❖ Human Being/Culminating/Achieving/Attaining/ Wholeness.

Language

The Chinese language is pictographic rather than alphabetic. Especially in ancient Chinese seal writing, the forms of Chinese characters resemble the realities to which they are referring. Many characters have come down to present time unchanged, however, many also are appearing in differing form due to changes in the Chinese language, different writing mediums and instruments, transcribing errors and interpolations and attempts to standardize the language.

Deeper and more extended meanings of Chinese characters are given etymologically through their radicals and phonetics and linguistically through their usages and variations. The Chinese characters do not grammatically distinguish nouns and verbs, singular and plural or tense, voice and gender and, as such, allow for great freedom in translating, interpreting and expressing meanings.

In this rendition, plurals, the present tense, active voice, the gerund form (-ing) and the modifier 'being' are used to avoid gender distinctions and to provide a sense of immediacy and action, e.g., a sentence like 'The sage was real when he instructed the student' is changed to 'Sages are being real when they are instructing students'.

Themes

The narratives of *The Lieh Tzu* text focus on the realities and actualities of the ordinary and everyday experiences of human being and living, e.g.:

Issues of:

Difficulties/problems/troubles/obstacles/struggles/burdens/toils/mistakes.

Anxiety/tension/stress/pressure/doubt/worry/fear/frustration/anger/revenge.

Shame/guilt/failure/loss/sorrow/misery/suffering/illness/declining/death.

States of:

Calm/quiet/peace/balance/equality/harmony/simplicity/sufficiency/comfort.

Freedom/liberation/carefreeness/enjoyment/happiness/joyfulness/contentment.

Understanding/friendship/communication/transforming/transcending/enlightenment.

Qualities/activities of:

Honesty/integrity/virtue/humility/trust/being true to one's inner nature/self/heart.

Spirit/energy/inner being/naturalness/illumination/enlightenment/awakening.

Clearness/emptiness/stillness/interconnectedness/merging/oneness/nonduality.

Accepting/letting-be/yielding/letting-go/non-thinking/non-knowing/non-doing.

Following natural laws/order/ways/changes/unfolding/proceeding/courses/cycles.

Non-investment in/non-attachment to/non-involvement in affairs/outcomes.

Non-controlling/non-directing/non-manipulating/non-forcing activities/behaviors.

Non-compliance with the conventions/norms/opinions and expectations of others.

Non-interest in the external appearances/value judgments/differences of others.

Non-pursuing of name/fame/status/rank/reputation/fortune/wealth/worth/power.

Accepting the uncontrollable/unpredictable/unexplainable workings of destiny/luck.

Understanding that success may be due to coincidences and not talent/skill/ability.

Living a dedicated life of studying/learning/teaching/training/practicing/cultivating.

While the originating, changing, transforming and resulting effects of the unitings and separatings of Yin/Yang Ch'i energies are only mentioned in several narratives throughout *The Lieh Tzu* text, many narratives are replete with references to numerous bipolar interrelationships, e.g.:

Heaven-Earth/Spirit-mind/mind-body/self-other/self-world/destiny-endeavor.

Reality-dream/awake-dreaming/real-artificial/wisdom-foolishness/teacher-student.

Constancy-transiency/growing-declining/health-illness/coming-going/living-dying.

Cause-effect/action-reaction/cause-symptom/push-pull/yielding-resisting/soft-rigid.

Good-bad/right-wrong/true-false/weak-strong/success-failure/gain-loss/fortune-misfortune.

Experiential Concepts

The following are characteristics, attributes, qualities and activities of eight principal experiential concepts and several others of the ancient Chinese Spiritual and philosophical tradition and way of being and living of Taoism that occur throughout *The Lieh Tzu* text.

TAO - ***Ultimate Reality of*****/as *Tao.***

1. Ultimate Reality/Origin/Source/Absolute/Essence.
2. No-Thing/Everything/Infinity/Eternity/Destiny.
3. Ubiquity/constancy/unity/identity.
4. Formlessness/namelessness/ineffability.
5. Universe/Heaven-Earth/Nature/human beings/all beings/things.
6. Uncreated/unborn/undying/independent/unconditioned.
7. Transcendent/immanent/nonpersonal/transpersonal/personal/interpersonal.
8. All That Is/As It Is/Everywhere At Once/Here And Now.
9. The natural law/order of beings/things.

TE - ***Potent Virtuosity of*****/as *Tao.***

1. Innate Tao-Nature.
2. Unique individualizing.
3. Efficacious power.
4. Virtuosity/genius.
5. Integrity/character/excellence.
6. Gifts/talents/abilities.
7. Inner reality/truth.
8. The natural integrity of beings/things.

CH'I - ***Cosmic/Vital Energy of*****/as *Tao.***

1. Primordial/acquired.
2. Nonmaterial/material.
3. Undifferentiated/differentiated.
4. Coalescing/dispersing/circulating.

5. Animating/activating/vitalizing.
6. Pervading/constituting/nourishing/sustaining.
7. Endowed/cultivated.
8. The natural energies of beings/things.

YIN/YANG CH'I - *Dynamic Bipolarity of*/as *Tao.*

1. Bipolarity/mutuality/complementarity/equality.
2. Interdependence/interacting/interchanging.
3. Changing/transforming/transmuting.
4. Alternating/reciprocating/exchanging.
5. Compensating/counterbalancing/centering.
6. Emptying/voiding/'zero-ing'.
7. Reversing.
8. The natural changes of beings/things.

WU WEI CH'I - *Kinetic Fluidity of*/as *Tao.*

1. Flowing/coursing/streaming.
2. Circulating/cycling.
3. Rotating/revolving/orbiting.
4. Tao-sourced activity.
5. Natural unfolding/proceeding/developing/progressing.
6. Frictionless/seamless/effortless.
7. Unmotivated/unplanned/unforced activity.
8. Returning.
9. The natural course of beings/things.

TZU JAN - *Natural Spontaneity of*/as *Tao.*

1. Self-so/self-like.
2. Of-itself-so/as-such.
3. Just-so/as-is.
4. Presencing.
5. Spontaneity.
6. Naturalness.
7. Freedom.
8. The natural presencing of beings/things.

WAN WU - ***Phenomenal Totality of/*****as** ***Tao.***

1. 10,000/myriad beings/things.
2. Innumerable/countless/incalculable.
3. Phenomenological objectivity.
4. Variety/diversity.
5. Multiplicity/plurality.
6. Totality/entirety/all beings/things.
7. Immanency/intimacy of Tao.
8. The natural forms of beings/things.

TAO JEN - ***Consummate Humanity of/*****as** ***Tao.***

1. Sacred/wise human beings (Lao Tzu).
2. True/free human beings (Chuang Tzu).
3. Real/practical human beings (Lieh Tzu).
4. Tao-focused/centered/realized/actualized.
5. Tao-returned/identified/Tao-like/Being-Tao.
7. Embodying/personifying/assimilating/enacting Tao.
8. Fulfilled/concluded/completed/consummated/ culminated.
9. The natural being/living of human beings.

Heaven

❖ celestial nature/spaciousness/head-centered.

Earth

❖ terrestrial nature/groundedness/belly-centered.

Human Being

❖ existential nature/centeredness/heart-centered.

Clearness

❖ mental concept/content-free/Tao-sourced 'knowing'.

Emptiness

❖ emotional desire/goods-free/Tao-sourced 'having'.

Stillness

❖ volitional purpose/deed-free/Tao-sourced 'doing'.

Oneness

❖ relational separation/other-free/Tao-sourced 'being'.

Letting-Be

❖ non-construing phenomena into mental 'contents'.
❖ non-abstracting/defining/naming/categorizing.
❖ non-rejecting/altering/revising.
❖ accepting/acknowledging/appreciating.
❖ regarding/respecting/receiving.

Letting-Go

❖ non-retaining experiences into emotional 'goods'.
❖ non-investing/attaching/selecting/preferring.
❖ non-collecting/claiming/owning.
❖ aligning/attuning/according.
❖ reflecting/relinquishing/reversing.

Going-With

❖ non-reacting activities into volitional 'deeds'.
❖ non-resisting/hindering/countering/conflicting.
❖ non controlling/directing/forcing.
❖ allowing/accomodating/accompanying.
❖ responding/replying/returning.

Being-With

❖ non-separating relationships into relational 'others'.
❖ non-distancing/isolating/dividing/excluding.
❖ non-alienating/negating/eliminating.
❖ affiliating/allying/abiding.
❖ rejoining/reconnecting/residing.

Metaphors

The various characters portrayed in the narratives of *The Lieh Tzu* text can be taken as metaphors for our various human natures as follows:

Immortals
❖ our divine/superhuman nature.

Sages/Masters/philosophers
❖ our awakened/wise nature.

Teachers/scholars/students
❖ our teaching/learning nature.

Sorcerers/physicians/patients
❖ our healing/curing nature.

Hermits/recluses/wanderers
❖ our solitary/wayfaring nature.

Emperors/kings/princes/lords/marquises/earls/noblemen/advisors
❖ our governing nature.

Ministers/diplomats/legislators/officials/bureaucrats/politicians
❖ our political nature.

Fathers/sons/brothers/wives/families
❖ our immediate familial nature.

Friends/neighbors/old/rich/poor men
❖ our everyday/social nature.

Masters/servants/caretakers
❖ our domestic/serving nature.

Musicians/singers/sculptor
❖ our masterful artistic nature.

Archers/acrobats/charioteer/breeder/trainer/apprentices
❖ our masterful skilled nature.

Ferryman/swimmers/fisherman
❖ our masterful talented nature.

Craftsperson/woodcutter/farmer/innkeeper
❖ our masterful occupational nature.

Confucius

❖ our benevolent/righteous/proper nature.

Lao Tzu/Wen Tzu/Chuang Tzu/Hu Tzu/Lieh Tzu/Yang Chu

❖ our Taoist-being nature.

Issues

The four principal experiential concepts of Te, Yin/Yang Ch'i, Wu Wei Ch'i and Tao can be respectively related and applied to the characteristics, attributes, qualities and activities of four common issues of ignorance, attachment, error and separation that can create and constitute problems and difficulties in the nature of real living as follows:

CONCEPT — *Te*

Unique individuality/Potent Virtuosity.

MODALITY

Knowing/noetic/cognitive/thinking/mentation.

STATE

Letting-Be/non-knowing of mental 'contents'/
Tao – 'knowing'.

ISSUE

Ignorance/non-acknowledging/non-accepting/non-appreciating of real living.

ACTIVITIES

1. Externalizing/abstracting/construing/analyzing/interpreting.
2. Presupposing/preconceiving/projecting/altering/distorting.
3. Imagining/fantasizing/idealizing/dreaming/deluding.
4. Misperceiving/misconceiving/misunderstanding/misinterpreting.
5. Defining/naming/labeling/determining/concluding.
6. Classifying/categorizing/comparing/contrasting/confusing.

7. Opining/hypothesizing/supposing/predicting/prognosticating.
8. Intellectualizing/rationalizing/justifying/falsifying/denying.
9. Omniscience/reifying/dogmatizing/formalizing/ritualizing.

CONCEPT — ***Yin/Yang Ch'i***

Dynamic bipolarity/Interdependent complementarity.

MODALITY

Having/dynamic/affective/feeling/emotion.

STATE

Letting-Go/non-having of emotional 'goods'/
Tao – 'having'.

ISSUE

Attachment/non-aligning with/non-attuning to/
non-according with real living.

ACTIVITIES

1. Attracting/evaluating/judging/preferring/selecting.
2. Investing/needing/wanting/desiring/coveting.
3. Seeking/pursuing/obtaining/getting/acquiring.
4. Appropriating/possessing/owning/harboring/claiming.
5. Collecting/storing/stockpiling/amassing/hoarding.
6. Grabbing/clinging/holding/keeping/retaining.
7. Exhibiting/displaying/boasting/parading/flaunting.
8. Duality/unilaterality/onesidedness/partiality/favoritism.
9. Wealth/riches/gain/profit/property/possessions/valuables.

CONCEPT — ***Wu Wei Ch'i***

Kinetic fluidity/Tao-sourced activity.

MODALITY

Doing/kinetic/conative/acting/volition.

STATE

Going-With/non-doing of volitional 'deeds'/
Tao – 'doing'.

Issue

Error/non-allowing of/non-acceding to/non-accompanying of real living.

Activities

1. Asserting/imposing/aggressing/invading/violating.
2. Interfering/controlling/manipulating/directing/forcing.
3. Blocking/obstructing/impeding/hindering/hampering.
4. Resisting/reacting/rebelling/conflicting/contending.
5. Opposing/counteracting/competing/defeating/winning.
6. Striving/planning/strategizing/contriving/devising.
7. Fabricating/manufacturing/engineering/implementing/ executing.
8. Administrating/managing/governing/ruling/commanding.
9. Domineering/dominating/conquering/subjugating/ exploiting.

Concept — *Tao*

Ultimate Reality/Intimate actuality.

Modality

Being/ontic/unitive/relating/identification.

State

Being-With/non-being of relational 'others'/
Tao – 'being'.

Issue

Separation/non-affiliating with/non-allying with/ non-abiding in real living.

Activities

1. Externalizing/distancing/objectifying/alienating/ marginalizing.
2. Dividing/splitting/fragmenting/fractionating/isolating.
3. Dissociating/disconnecting/excluding/abandoning/ eliminating.
4. Neglecting/devaluing//depreciating/invalidating/ disqualifying.
5. Stereotyping/profiling/reducing/negating/nullifying.

6. Infantalizing/patronizing/stigmatizing/pathologizing/demonizing.
7. Depersonalizing/dehumanizing/criminalizing/victimizing.
8. Inauthenticity/facade/persona/unavailability/inaccessibility.
9. Status/reputation/name/fame/prestige/elitism/inflation.

Commentaries

Except for introductory and occasional interspersed and footnoted comments, the narratives of *The Lieh Tzu* text have not been systematically commentaried upon in the three English language translations cited in the references of this rendition. The psychotherapeutic commentaries of this rendition apply portions of each of the narratives to descriptions of the nature, characteristics, understandings, experiences and activities of real attenders conducting the attending relationship/process.

In companion books on Lao Tzu's *Tao Te Ching* and Chuang Tzu's *Nei P'ien*, so-called psychotherapists/counselors have been respectively considered as 'wise attenders' and 'true attenders' in keeping with textual identifications of Sacred/wise human beings/Sheng Jen and true/free human beings/Chen Jen. In this rendition, so-called psychotherapists/counselors are being considered as 'real attenders' in keeping with textual identifications of real/actual human beings/Shih Jen. So-called patients/counselees are simply referred to as 'human beings' and/or 'human beings engaged in the attending relationship/process'.

Psychotherapy is being considered, etymologically, as the Greek '*psyche-therapeuein*' or 'attending the Soul'. In the psychotherapeutic commentaries of this rendition, considering psychotherapy/counseling as the attending relationship/process is identifying it as a way of encouraging, supporting, assisting, facilitating, guiding and completing some of the psychological dimensions of the life-long journeying of our Human Soul as an embodied Spirit and inSpirited body. In the wayfaring journeying of our Human Soul, Tao/Ultimate Reality is considered as being identical with Spirit and Te/Virtuosity is considered as being identical with our Human Soul. Soul-work, Soul-making and the enSouling process are explicitly considered in *Lao Tzu's Tao Te Ching. Soul Journeying Commentaries. A Sojourning Pilgrim's Rendering of 81 Spirit Soul Passages.*

Each psychotherapeutic commentary can be a rich source of, and re-source for, deep intrapsychic and interpersonal awakening, experiencing and transforming. The essential realities and existential meanings of the commentaries can be internalized and assimilated when read openly and slowly; with slow, deep and full breathing and in calm meditative states of concentration, reflection, contemplation and absorption, i.e., in meditative focus, openness, awareness and identification.

On Attending

In the commentaries of this rendition, as noted above, instead of being named psychotherapists/counselors, the human beings engaged in the practice of psychotherapy/counseling are designated as 'real attenders' and psychotherapy/counseling is designated as the 'attending relationship/process'. This is consistent with the etymological meaning of psychotherapy as 'Soul' (Greek – *psyche*) 'attending' (Greek – *therapeuein*) and also is identical with Shih Jen/Real human beings nourishing, cultivating and sustaining Tao as our innermost, deepest, centermost, truest and utmost nature, i.e., Te/Virtuosity.

Attending is a fundamental quality and essential factor in the psychotherapy/counseling relationship/process.[8] Also, various forms and meanings of 'attending' denote states and activities of being and consciousness that apply to four principal experiential concepts identified in this rendition, integrating them and psychotherapy/counseling practice in the following ways:

Te

- ❖ in the letting-be/'knowing' mode of no-'thing' knowing *about*, or the construing *of*, mental object-'contents'.
- ❖ paying attention *to*/mindfully, availably and receptively observing/giving focused heed *to* the phenomena *of*/*in* conscious awareness.

Yin/Yang Ch'i

- ❖ in the letting-go/'having' mode of no-'thing' having *of*, or the attaching *to*, emotional object-'goods'.
- ❖ being attentive *to*/thoughtfully, sympathetically and kindly considering/caring *about*/empathizing *with* the needs/comfort *of* others.

Wu Wei Ch'i

- ❖ in the going-with/'doing' mode of no-'thing' doing *of*, or the performing *of*, volitional object-'deeds'.
- ❖ attending *to*/responsively, cooperatively and appropriately taking care *of* necessities requiring completing.

Tao

- ❖ in the being-with/'being' mode of no-'thing' being *of*, or the separating *of*, relational object-'others'.
- ❖ being an attender or an attendant present *at*/collectively joining/participating *in* a given place/occasion/event or looking *after*/staying *with* another as a companion/friend/professional or being concomitant *to*/associated *with*/resultant *of* circumstances.

Also, the various meanings of 'tending' have to do with awaiting, standing by, listening, watching over, caring for, serving, cultivating and fostering.

Real psychotherapists/counselors are human beings who are paying attention, being attentive and attending *to* as an attender present *at*, ready to serve and participating *in* the attending relationship/process and the attendant phenomena concomitantly associated *with* and accompanying it.

Ideally, these ways of real attending in psychotherapy/counseling involve the mental clearness, emotional emptiness, volitional stillness and relational oneness of psychotherapists/counselors and the human beings with whom they are meeting. These ways of attending can open the Way to co-creating and co-experiencing the unique individuality, equal reciprocity, appropriate activity and intimate intersubjectivity of the psychotherapy/counseling attending relationship/process; such that essential, necessary and appropriate actions and interactions naturally flow and organically follow from the clear and open awarenesses of, and the deep and full connections between, attending psychotherapists/counselors and human beings.

So, the healing and transforming potency, efficacy and intimacy of these ways of conducting the attending relationship/process are not only, or not so much, a matter of real attenders knowing psychological theories and concepts, making clinical assessments and judgments, devising treatment plans and intervention strategies and utilizing psychotherapy techniques and methods as they are the Spirit in which they are brought into it; the ways of being that they are bringing to it and the openness, clearness, deepness, fullness and connectedness of their presentness *in* it and their attentiveness *to* it.

Real human living is the attentive experiencing of self-awakening, transforming and developing that is equivalent to the journeying of our Human Souls from ego-identifying with body, mind, others and the world to Self-identifying with Spirit, Psyche/Consciousness, fellow Human Beings and the Multiverse; the wayfaring from the '10,000 things' to Tao. The attending relationship/process of psychotherapy/counseling is one beneficial way of attending to, encouraging, supporting, assisting, facilitating and guiding at least some part of the natural unfolding of the wayfaring journey returning us Home to our Human Selves, Souls and Spirit.

Rendition

This rendition of *The Lieh Tzu* is not a translation of the text but is, rather, like the renditions of its two companion books, Lao Tzu's *Tao Virtuosity Experience* and Chuang Tzu's *Seven Interior Records*, the literary equivalent of a jazz rendition primarily characterized by interpretive solo improvisations that depart from a musical composition as originally scored.

The narratives of the three translations of *The Lieh Tzu* text listed in the references of this rendition have been closely read, thoroughly studied, cross-referenced, correlated and reflected upon and are distilled, condensed and paraphrased renderings of each one of the narratives. The basic structure of the text is followed in that its eight sections are retained, however, each section and its narratives are retitled based upon an interpretation of their principal focus and contents.

Poetic license has been exercised in titling *The Lieh Tzu* text as *The Nature of Real Living/Hsing Shih Sheng* since, of all of the three foundational texts of ancient Chinese philosophical Taoism (the other two being *The Tao Te Ching* and *The Chuang Tzu*), it most focuses upon the actual and practical realities of everyday living. The title also reflects the enduring Spirit of Lieh Tzu as it is retrospectively projected into the narratives over the years by the compilers of *The Lieh Tzu* text.

For ease of reading and for facilitating making generalizations, commentaries and applications; the Chinese names of principal characters and locations have been eliminated, along with the actual dialogues between principals in each narrative. Each narrative is a present tense rendering of its essential story line and, in some narratives, the gender of the characters has been changed to include women. Readers are encouraged to peruse the referenced translations for specifics of the narratives.

The one-hundred eleven narratives of this rendition follow those of the Wong explication where some of them that appear in *The Chuang Tzu* text have been eliminated along with some that are considered to be of minor significance or limited relevance.[9]

Each narrative is followed by its corresponding psychotherapeutic commentary wherein psychotherapy/counseling is referred to as 'the attending relationship/process', psychotherapists/counselors are referred to as 'real attenders' and patients/counselees are referred to as 'human beings' or 'human beings engaged in the attending relationship/process'. Quick references to the essential message of each one of the narratives and commentaries comprise Appendixes One and Two.

The central themes and commentaries of the rendition are based upon: 1) studying numerous writings in the Spiritual literature of Chinese Taoist Philosophy/Tao Chia and Religion/Chiao; 2)consulting Chinese language dictionaries and reference materials for the etymological definitions and extended meanings of many of the Chinese characters; 3) workshop experiences with several Tao-Masters and 4) teaching, training, supervising, mentoring and practicing in the field of psychotherapy/counseling in a wide variety of academic institutions, inpatient and outpatient clinical treatment facilities and counseling centers and group and individual private practice settings during the past fifty-seven years.

This work, like its previous ones on Lao Tzu's *Tao Te Ching* and Chuang Tzu's *Nei P'ien*, is not intended to be about Chinese Taoism as yet another 'ism-ology', school or way of psychotherapy involving particular theoretical concepts and methodological techniques for use in treating specific clinical conditions or patient populations. Rather, it is, at the very most, a westernized urban neo-Taoist way of really and actually understanding and conducting any psychotherapy/counseling relationship/process that integrates Eastern psychospiritual and Western psychotherapeutic personal and transpersonal attitudes and approaches, regardless of particular theoretical orientations or methodological applications.

Also, this rendition is not an owner's operational/'how to do' manual for psychotherapy practice since, in general, it does not include concrete and detailed examples of specific interpretations, interactions and interventions in the attending relationship/process. The greatest emphasis of psychotherapeutic agency, potency, efficacy and intimacy is upon the natural, integral and practical modes, states and qualities of the Tao-identified being, awakened consciousness, clear awareness, full attention and deep connection of real attenders rather than upon any particular kinds of theoretical conceptions entertained, interpersonal relationships engaged in or methodological procedures utilized, e.g.,

Te/Virtuosity

- ❖ mode of attending/attention to/heeding of phenomena.
- ❖ state of nondual awakeness/awareness/accepting/acknowledging.
- ❖ state of letting-be/individuality/uniqueness/integrity/receiving.
- ❖ mode of 'knowing'/clearness/consciousness/openness of mind.
- ❖ qualities of non-externalizing/abstracting/objectifying.
- ❖ qualities of non-presupposing/preconceiving/predefining.
- ❖ qualities of non-portending/interrogating/interdicting/interjecting.
- ❖ quality of intersubjective interpreting/interpretations.

Yin/Yang Ch'i

- ❖ mode of attending/attentive to/caring for needs.
- ❖ state of empathic attuning/adjusting/aligning/according.
- ❖ state of letting-go/alternating/balancing/voiding/reversing.
- ❖ mode of 'having'/emptiness/centeredness/equalness of heart.
- ❖ qualities of non-assessing/evaluating/desiring.
- ❖ qualities of non-prejudging/preferring/pre-empting.
- ❖ qualities of non-extending/interpolating/interposing/interceding.
- ❖ quality of interdependent interchanging/interchanges.

Wu Wei Ch'i

- mode of attending/attending to/taking care of business.
- state of synergic entraining/acceding/allowing/accompanying.
- state of going-with/sourcing/yielding/following/returning.
- mode of 'doing'/stillness/cooperativeness/calmness of will.
- qualities of non-controlling/manipulating/forcing.
- qualities of non-preplanning/predetermining/prefabricating.
- qualities of non-intending/interfering/interrupting/intercepting.
- quality of interactive intervening/interventions.

Tao/Ultimacy

- mode of attending/attendance at/participating in events.
- state of co-existing beingness/affiliating/allying/abiding.
- state of being-with/joining/communing/uniting/residing.
- mode of 'being'/oneness/connectedness/wholeness of being.
- qualities of non-separating/alienating/fragmenting.
- qualities of non-precedence/pre-eminence/precluding.
- qualities of non-pretending/intermixing/interlocking/interfusing.
- quality of interrelated interconnecting/interconnections.

Rather, this rendition and commentaries are, purely and simply, an opportunity to express some of whatever observations, discoveries and connections have been made during sixty-two years of integrating the psychospiritual and psychotherapeutic attitudes and approaches of the disciplines of ancient Chinese Taoism and modern Western Psychology.

As mentioned above, the narratives and commentaries of the rendition are best read with slow, deep and full breathing and in a state of quiet relaxation and open awareness, i.e., with a relatively clear mind, empty heart, still will and free Spirit, so as to allow their meanings to resonate more deeply and fully in your unique inner being and for your individual journeying and intimate wayfaring along the wilderness pathways, flowing watercourses and awaiting frontiers of Tao.

Once again, as with the rendering of, and psychotherapeutic commentaries on, Lao Tzu's *Tao Te Ching/Tao Virtuosity Experience* and Chuang Tzu's *Nei P'ien/Seven Interior Records* texts; if you find this material to be of some, or any, interest, value, inspiration, encouragement, support, assistance, guidance, use and/or benefit to you in awakening, discovering, experiencing, understanding and sharing your precious human being, conscious human living and unique wayfaring journeying; I am infinitely pleased and eternally grateful.

Raymond Bart Vespe
Santa Rosa, California
Autumnal Equinox, 2016

SECTION ONE

THE NATURE OF ORIGINATING/HEAVEN'S BESTOWAL

INTRODUCTION

THE NARRATIVES OF SECTION ONE FOCUS ON:

1. THE ORIGINAL NO-THINGNESS OF UNBORN TAO.
2. THE ORIGINATING NON-ULTIMATE/WU CHI.
3. THE UNDIFFERENTIATED/FORMLESS/ONENESS OF PRIMORDIAL CH'I/YUAN CH'I ENERGY.
4. YIN/YANG CH'I TRANSFORMING ENERGIES AND THE INTERCONNECTEDNESS OF ALL THINGS.
5. HEAVEN-EARTH/NATURE/UNIVERSE/SPIRIT/HUMAN BEING/ALL THINGS.
6. EMPTINESS/STILLNESS/LETTING-BE/HAPPINESS.
7. THE NATURAL WAY/ORDER OF THE UNIVERSE.
8. THE LIFE COURSE/CYCLE OF BIRTHING/GROWING/DECAYING/DYING.
9. NO CONTROL OVER DESTINY AND THE WORKINGS OF HEAVEN-EARTH.
10. LIFE/BODY/MIND/SELF/BEING/SOUL/SPIRIT/PROGENY AS LOANED BY HEAVEN-EARTH.

YUAN

原

ORIGIN/SOURCE
SPRING/FOUNTAINHEAD
PRIMARY/ROOT CAUSE
BEGINNING
ORIGINAL/NATURAL
TRULY/ACTUALLY

YUAN

元

ORIGINAL/FIRST
HEAD/CHIEF
PRIMARY/FIRST CAUSE
ANCIENT/BEGINNING
FUNDAMENTAL/BASIC
PRINCIPAL/PRINCIPLE

THE ORIGIN

WU	**CHI**
無	極
No-/not-non-/un- Without Nothing/No-'thing'	Ultimate Apex/zenith/summit Utmost/extreme/limit
CH'I	**LIANG**
氣	良
Breath/cosmic/vital energy Air/vapor/ether/gas/steam/smoke Primordial/nonmaterial/ undifferentiated Acquired/material/differentiated Animating/activating/vitalizing Life-constituting/pervading/ sustaining	Heavenly bestowal/gift Nature of human being Natural gifts Good/goodness/fine Virtuous/kindhearted Sagacious/peaceful

THE NON-ULTIMATE/CH'I ENERGY

Heaven's bestowal of the Primordial/Cosmic Energy of the universe and of the endowed/life force of human beings, all beings and things.

Narrative 1
Everything from No-thing

Lieh Tzu is moving to another state and students are gathered around requesting some parting words of wisdom learned from his own teacher. He encourages them to learn from the orderly course that Heaven/T'ien and Earth/Ti and Nature follow and to let everything go naturally according to its uniquely individual nature and way. He indicates that students who are less dependent upon external supports might adjust to his absence better but that more dependent ones have their place and play their part in the co-creating and comings and goings of human living and should be allowed to develop at their own rate, in their own time and in their own way.

Lieh Tzu reminds students of writings in *The Book of the Yellow Emperor* that the unborn, unchanging and undying Valley Spirit/Mysterious Female is the undifferentiated, boundless and limitless No-thingness /Wu Chi and the originating and creative source of Heaven-Earth, endless alternating Yin/Yang Ch'i changes and all living beings and is their inexhaustible sustaining resource of primordial vital energy/Yuan Ch'i. He adds by saying that most of our human birthing, living, changing, growing, declining and dying is part of the workings of Heaven-Earth, the natural order of things and the way of Tao that are fundamentally, essentially and ultimately beyond our conscious control.

Commentary 1 ❖ Everything from No-thing

Real attenders are:

1. Appreciating the Mysterious originating of human beings engaged in the attending relationship/process; are accepting and supporting their uniquely individualized natures and lives; and are allowing and facilitating their uniquely individualized places and parts in the whole natural order of things.

2. Assisting and guiding human beings in attuning to and according with the inexhaustible source and resources of their vital energy/Ch'i and in understanding and yielding to the reality that many of the natural processes and much of the natural unfolding of their human life course, life cycle and lifespan may fundamentally, essentially and ultimately be beyond their conscious control.

Narrative 2
Everything is Interconnected

Lieh Tzu continues by saying that the interacting of Yin/Yang Ch'i energies characterizes the production, nature and changes of Heaven and Earth, human beings and things and that they all originate from the same one ultimateless and formless Non-being of the Great Void/Wu Chi through four stages of cosmogonic sequencing, i.e.,

1. Yuan Ch'i/the Great Monad/Primordial Ch'i/undivided/undifferentiated.
2. Yin and Yang/the Great Dyad/Yin-Yang Ch'i/Heaven above/Earth below.
3. Wu Chi + Yin/Yang Ch'i/Ta'i Chi/the Great Triad/Heaven/Earth/Human Being.
4. Wan Wu/the Great Myriad/the '10,000 things'/their essences/forms/qualities.

All things are originated by, connected with and manifestations of one undifferentiated Origin and are differentiated from and interconnected and interwoven with each other.

Commentary 2 ❖ Everything is Interconnected

Real attenders are:

1. Aware of the reality that all phenomena of human being, existing, living and experiencing originate in the one

formless, non-objectifiable, nondual and undifferentiated Source of Tao/ Wu Chi and, as such, are equal and interconnected in their lives and in the lives of human beings engaged in the attending relationship/process and in its life as well.

2. Experiencing that such myriad and diverse phenomena arising from Original Tao do so through the ongoing alternating, reciprocating, transforming and reversing of the interacting dynamics of Yin Ch'i and Yang Ch'i energies and, as such, are interrelated and interchangeable.

Narrative 3
Heaven and Earth

Lieh Tzu says that, even though Heaven and Earth create our human existence, they are not omnipotent and that, even though sages are models for our human lives, they are not omniscient. He continues by saying that Heaven, Earth and sages each fulfill their respective functions of sheltering, supporting and educating; are interdependent with, complementary to and counterbalancing of each other; without one being more valuable or worthy than the other.

Lieh Tzu says that the workings of Heaven and Earth follow the alternating process of Yin Ch'i and Yang Ch'i and the vocations of sages follow the constant principle of Virtuosity and impartiality. All of the myriad phenomena of human being, existing, living and experiencing are bipolar in nature, e.g., creators and the created, birthers and the birthed, sustainers and the sustained, completers and the completed; and that, while their beings and forms are objectified, their origin is non-objectifiable and without being, knowing or doing anything. Identifying *as* this non-being/Wu Yu, non-knowing/Wu Chih and non-doing/Wu Wei enables human beings to be both forms of bipolarities without mutually exclusive either-or duality, contradiction, opposition, conflict, conditions or limits.

Commentary 3 ❖ Heaven and Earth

Real attenders are:

1. Aware that Heaven, Earth, sages and master psychotherapists are not all-powerful and all-knowing and that they themselves and human beings engaged in the attending relationship/process each have their unique and equally valuable places and play their unique and equally worthy parts in the overall natural way of Tao, the universe and things.
2. Identifying *as* the non-being, non-knowing and non-doing of Original Tao and are equally and impartially experiencing the bipolarity and fluidity of all phenomena occurring in the attending relationship/process as they are objectified within their conscious awareness and experience and that of human beings engaged in the attending relationship/process.[10]

Narrative 4
Living and Dying

Lieh Tzu is journeying from his home state to a neighboring state and on the way comes across a one-hundred year old human skull lying beside the road. He picks up the skull, brushes it off, looks at it for awhile, sets it back down and then asks it whether it is unfortunate to be dead and he is fortunate to be alive or whether it is fortunate to be dead and he is unfortunate to be alive.

Lieh Tzu asks that what is there to gain in living or to lose in dying when in the end, after our one-hundred years, we will all be a pile of bones? Living is not the beginning of things and dying is not the ending of things, all things come and go naturally, living does not go on forever and living and dying are both natural parts of the life course and life cycle; so why be happy or sad about either? Seeing through the illusion of living and dying is being identified with the eternity of Heaven, Earth and the universe.

Commentary 4 ❖ Living and Dying

Real attenders are:

1. Accepting the transiency of human living and the initiating, duration and terminating of the attending relationship/process with impartiality and equanimity.
2. Identifying *as* the timelessness of Heaven, Earth, the universe and Eternal Tao and are seeing through and being beyond the illusions of beginnings and endings and living and dying.

Narrative 5
Originating and Returning

Lieh Tzu says that all things come from and return to the same one Origin and that so-called beginnings are only the gathering, condensing and coalescing of vital energy/Ch'i and so-called endings are only its dispersing, dissolving and dissipating. All things are interconnected and produce effects on their counterparts, like light and shadow, sound and echo. Beginnings can be endings and endings can be beginnings and who is to say which is which?

Lieh Tzu says that living and dying follow a natural course and that we should let both come and go as they do without trying to rush or delay either one. What must come and go will come and go without our trying to make things happen or not happen. The living of our Spirit and body is a creation of the uniting of Heaven and Earth and when the two are separated in dying, each returns to its source, the Spiritual Soul/Hun ascending back to Heaven and the physical Soul/P'o descending back to Earth. The ending of our wayfaring and sojourning in the human life course and life cycle is a returning homecoming and a new beginning.

Commentary 5 ❖ Originating and Returning

Real attenders are:

1. Aware that beginnings and endings are interconnected counterparts and that their living, that of human beings engaged in the attending relationship/process and the initiating of the attending relationship/process are the differentiating and joining of primordial energy/Yuan Ch'i descending from Heaven, ascending from Earth and uniting as human being and interbeing and are an ending of 'then' and all that came before in the past and a new beginning of 'now' and all that is to come after in the future.
2. Aware that endings and beginnings are interconnected counterparts and that their dying, that of human beings engaged in the attending relationship/process and the terminating of the attending relationship/process are the separating and dissipating of vital energies/Yin-Yang Ch'i ascending back to Heaven, descending back to Earth and disuniting as human being and interbeing and also are an ending of 'then' and all that came before in the past and a new beginning of 'now' and all that is to come after in the future.

Narrative 6
Stages of Vital Energy

Lieh Tzu divides the human life course and life span into four periods of infancy, youth, old age and death. Vital energy/Ch'i is plentiful, strong and harmonious in infancy; intense, volatile and competetive in youth; weakening, declining and relaxing in old age and stilled, absent and returned in death.

Lieh Tzu says that these are four periods that human beings must pass through and accept their changes as natural stages of the developmental sequencing of vital energy/Ch'i throughout the human life cycle of living, growing, declining and dying.

Commentary 6 ❖ Stages of Vital Energy

Real attenders are:

1. Experiencing that the life course and developmental growth of the attending relationship/process usually go through four stages of its infancy, youth, maturity and termination that can be respectively and roughly characterized as strong and harmonious, unstable and conflicted, relaxed and accepting and concluded and completed.
2. Understanding and accepting the changes in vital energy/Ch'i that accompany the four stages in the life span of the attending relationship/process as they naturally occur and manifest in the behaviors, activities and interactions of human beings engaged in it.

Narrative 7
Spectrum of Happiness

Confucius is passing through a village and notices a wayfarer happily wandering about, playing a lute and singing. He inquires about the reasons for the man's happiness and is told by him that his happiness is due to being a human being blessed with wisdom, a man socially favored over women, a healthy man older in years and a simple man unafraid of being poor and of dying.

Confucius is on the way to a neighboring state and meets a hermit who is at least a hundred years old and who is happily singing as he is scavenging grain. A student sympathizes with the old man whom he perceives as toiling and tired but is told by him that he is not to be pitied because he is happy that he is alive, healthy, single, worry free at his age and considering dying as a return and possibly a better rebirth.

A student of Confucius is wanting to take a rest from his demanding studies but is told by him that there is no rest except in death and that some people are happy to die because it is a liberation from the hard work of cultivating and making a living; is the ending of a life-long journey of desiring and straying from their original and true nature and is an easy and restful homecoming or a finding of their way back and returning home.

Commentary 7 ❖ Spectrum of Happiness

Real attenders are:

1. Appreciating that happiness in living has to do with being grateful for a human incarnation, good health, gender equality, long life and few worries of poverty and mortality.
2. Acknowledging that human living and psychotherapeutic work are ongoing, often difficult and without respite or relief except for the liberation and happiness of completing and terminating; the ending of being lost, desiring and seeking and the coming home to, and residing in, one's original and true inner Tao-nature/Virtuosity.

Narrative 8
Emptiness and Stillness

Lieh Tzu is asked why he values emptiness and replies that it is liberating to be free of attachments to accomplishments, recognition, approval and praise and their attendant worries. He continues that accomplishments are not completely of one's own doing and involve the workings of Heaven and Earth and the coincidence of many favorable conditions.

Lieh Tzu adds by saying that seeing the emptiness and non-having of things assist in cultivating stillness and the non-doing of things and avoid trouble and losing one's way, oneself and Tao.

Chuang Tzu tells of two persons who both lose a sheep. One becomes depressed over the misfortune and loses himself in depravities because of being so attached to loss. The other one uses the misfortune to find herself in opportunities because she is not attached to loss.

Commentary 8 ❖ Emptiness and Stillness

Real attenders are:

1. Empty of investments in, attachments to and preferences for particular concepts and theories, agendas and

strategies, methods and techniques, objectives and goals, results and outcomes, etc. in their reflections, interpretations, responses, interventions, relationships and interactions with human beings.

2. Free of attachments to success or failure, gain or loss, and are understanding that any positive accomplishments in the attending relationship/process are not only of their own doing and involve the coincidence, concurrence, conjunction, convergence and confluence of a variety of causative influences, e.g., the providence, grace and guidance of Heaven-Earth's working; potential readiness, suitable circumstances, favorable conditions and appropriate timing and the No-thing 'doing' of Tao-sourced activity.

Narrative 9
Growing and Decaying

Lieh Tzu says that Heaven, Earth and human beings are constantly changing but that their changes are often so slow, gradual and subtle that many go unnoticed. What rises and grows in living is naturally balanced by falling and decaying. Living continues naturally and is maintained by our not interfering with or trying to control it by accelerating and forcing growing or delaying and preventing decaying. The constant growing, changing and decaying of living processes are often only observed after a long absence or when inferred after the fact from end results.

Commentary 9 ❖ Growing and Decaying

Real attenders are:

1. Experiencing that human beings are constantly changing naturally, are observing their often subtle changes and are not trying to cause or modify changes in their thinking, feeling, behaving and energy or to control, force, accelerate or delay them through purposely motivated and strategically

implemented interfering manipulations and interactions.
2. Aware of the natural compensating and counterbalancing of the changes that human beings undergo and are accepting and acknowledging, attuning to and according with and allowing and accompanying the dynamics and kinetics of Yin/Yang Ch'i and Wu Wei Ch'i energies as they naturally reverse bipolarity and return to origins without intervening, except when absolutely essential, necessary and/or appropriate.

Narrative 10
Vapor and Soil

An old man is afraid that the sky will fall down and the ground will break up and that he will not escape dying. A friend reassures him that the sky is lightly condensed vapor and the ground is solidly compacted soil that have been present and sustaining living for a very long time.

A hermit, hearing of the old man's fears, says that Heaven and Earth accumulate the vapors of the sky and the soil of the ground and their mysterious workings often produce transient things, so why could or might not the sky evaporate or the ground disintegrate at some time in the future.

Lieh Tzu says that we do not really know the ultimate fate of Heaven and Earth's creations and destructions and cannot really do anything about them anyway. So, forget worrying about safety and security in terms of possible catastrophic events that may or may not occur in the future. While we are living, we do not know what it really is like to be dead and vice versa.

Commentary 10 ❖ Vapor and Soil

Real attenders are:

1. Not wasting precious life time and energy worrying or catastrophizing about possible future events, such as

whether or not the protective cover of Heaven or the supportive ground of Earth will continue to exist, over which human beings have no control or about which human beings can do nothing anyway.

2. Using any apparently abstract future concerns, worries, anxieties and fears of human beings as metaphors of, and openings into exploring, their present concerns, worries, anxieties and fears regarding vulnerability and basic safety and security in their concrete surroundings and relationships which they are experiencing as being beyond their power to control.

Narrative 11
Borrowed Wealth

A ruler asks his minister whether he, the ruler, can possess the ways and powers of Heaven and Earth and make them go according to his wishes and desires. The minister replies that the power and energy of that which has no beginning or ending cannot be possessed by thoughts of mind, feelings of heart, actions of will or relations of self. Human life is an effect, result and product and cannot create an originating source, like a shadow and echo cannot produce light and sound. Our life, body, mind, self, being, Soul, Spirit and progeny are not possessions of our own and are granted by, and on loan from, Heaven and Earth.

A very poor man visits a very rich man to see if he can learn ways to become wealthy and does so by what the rich man calls 'stealing'. However, the poor man is caught stealing and is severely punished. He accuses the rich man of deceiving him but the rich man clarifies that what he means by 'stealing' is misinterpreted. The rich man explains that what he calls 'stealing' is taking hold of the bounty of Heaven, Earth and Nature, e.g., sunlight, rainwater, rich soil, grown plants and forest animals, that is the possession or property of no one but is available and accessible to anyone and everyone.

A sage adds that the abundant blessings and gifts bestowed and endowed (en-Tao-ed) by the Yin/Yang Ch'i energies of Heaven, Earth and Tao are here to use for living, are not owned, can be borrowed and will be returned in some way or form at some point or moment in time.

Commentary 11 ❖ Borrowed Wealth

Real attenders are:

1. Understanding and appreciating that our human life, body, mind, being, self, Soul, Spirit and children are blessed gifts of Heavenly and Earthly Tao that are quintessentially and fundamentally on loan and are not possessions of our mentally 'knowing' minds, emotionally 'having' hearts, volitionally 'doing' wills and relationally 'being' selves.
2. Experiencing that, while the plentiful blessings and gifts bestowed and endowed by Heavenly and Earthly Tao through their creating, originating and generating energy and power cannot be produced or possessed by human beings; they can be humbly accepted on loan, gratefully borrowed from, respectfully made good use of for sustaining life and, at some point, inevitably returned, hopefully in good condition.

SECTION TWO
THE NATURE OF TRANSCENDING/YELLOW EMPEROR

INTRODUCTION

THE NARRATIVES OF SECTION TWO FOCUS ON:

1. Understanding the inner nature of beings and not focusing on external appearances.
2. According with/following the natural way/course of things.
3. Softness/yielding/trusting/not controlling/forcing/conflicting with things.
4. Regulating vital Ch'i energy/not displaying Virtuosity.
5. Stillness/inner calmness/letting-go/emptiness/simplicity.
6. Dissolving dualistic differences between outer and inner.
7. Harmonizing/becoming one with/merging with the Laws of Nature/the natural way.
8. Acting naturally without thinking/knowing/being self-conscious.
9. Superhuman abilities and immortality.

CH'AO

超

Transcend
Go before/go beyond
Step over/rise above
Exceed/surpass
Superior to
Supernatural
Ultra-/Super-/Extra-

SHANG

上

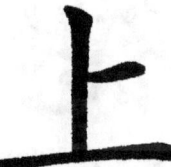

Ascend
Before/higher
Go up/upward
Above/over/summit
Superior/best
Essence
Supreme

TRANSCENDENCE

T'IEN

天

Heaven/sky
Celestial/firmament
Canopy/cover
Vast space
Nature (with earth)
Anthropomorphic diety

TI

地

Earth/soil
Terrestrial/land
Ground/support
Local place
Nature (with Heaven)
Situation/position

TE

德

Unique individuality
Integrity/character/inner truth
Goodness/kindness
Efficacious potency
Virtuosity/genius
Inborn Tao-nature

TSAI

在

Be/exist/be alive/present
Substance/constitution
Join/rest/remain with
Powers in natural activities
Endowments/gifts/genius
Innate talents/abilities

HEAVEN-EARTH/NATURE
AND
VIRTUOSITY/INNER TAO-NATURE

Narrative 12
The Dreamland of Immortality

The Yellow Emperor/Huang Ti surveys his country, is satisfied with his accomplishments and delighted with being respected and retires from governmental duties to enjoy himself. However, after indulging his senses for some time, he starts to decline physically and mentally and decides to return to exclusively ruling the country. But because of being so zealous, he again declines physically and mentally. He realizes that both indulging and over-working himself are not viable ways of living and takes some time out to quietly meditate.

In the process, Huang Ti dreams that he visits an immortal land, reached only by a Spirit journey, without rulers and teachers where everything follows its natural course and where everyone lives a fulfilling and peaceful life beyond dualities, needs and wants, judgments and preferences, differences and conflicts, anxieties and fears and the limitations of body-mind. The inhabitants of this immortal land are open, friendly, kind, gentle and helpful and are endowed with superhuman abilities, immunities and invulnerabilities.

Huang Ti emerges from his dream feeling that he is enlightened and that his enlightenment is due to stopping consciously thinking about what is the best way to cultivate and regulate himself. His subsequent enlightened ruling of the country results in it growing to become like the immortal land of his dream.

Commentary 12 ❖ The Dreamland of Immortality

Real attenders are:

1. Living and modeling for human beings a middle way of being between the extremes of either sensual indulging or stressful over-working, both of which result in ill-health and losses of physical, emotional, mental and Spiritual energy and well-being.
2. Open to meditatively journeying, experiencing and

residing in transcendent dimensions, realms and states of supramental, non-ordinary and enlightened consciousness that are inaccessible to/in ordinary space-time ego-limited conscious thinking but which can be useful for its transformative expansion, extension and manifestation in reality.

Narrative 13
Riding on the Wind

Lieh Tzu learns to ride on the wind and float on clouds from his immortal teacher and sage-friend. He is sought out by a wayfarer desiring to learn such skills who stays with Lieh Tzu for some time but leaves impatient and angry over being ignored and not taught anything. He calms down, realizes his impulsiveness and returns to Lieh Tzu asking to be his student again.

Lieh Tzu tells the wayfarer about the many years of arduous discipline involved and attainments required before finally being engaged by his teacher and then about the more years it took to experience nonduality, illumination, equanimity, the gathering of Spirit energy and the dissolving of his bodily form such that he became light enough to be carried by the wind and float on clouds. The wayfarer realizes that he is not fit for the requirements of learning and abandons his project.

Commentary 13 ❖ Riding on the Wind

Real attenders are:

1. Experiencing that learning the skills required for transcending the limitations of ego-identifying and mastering the abilities necessary for Spiritual journeying involve intensive and extensive disciplining, training and practicing.
2. Realizing that only a few human beings engaged in the attending relationship/process are interested in, ready for, fit for or capable of making and keeping a sustained commitment to the arduous discipline and diligent effort

involved in transcending the ego-limitations of body-mind.

Narrative 14
Oneness and Merging

Lieh Tzu asks the sage Wen Tzu about how enlightened human beings can stay under water and not drown, walk on fire and not burn and float on air and not fall. The sage answers that they do so not by any skill but by gathering and focusing Spirit energy. They see through the differing external qualities and appearances of things, realize that they all come from the same one Origin and can merge with them. They become one with water, fire and air and do not drown, burn or fall.

Wen Tzu continues by saying that enlightened human beings wander and reside in originating Non-Being, the realm where there is no beginning or ending and where the myriad things appear and disappear. They purify their Original Tao-nature, cultivate their Ch'i energy and maintain their Virtuosity. They are unified with the natural laws and merged with the natural order of things and their Spirit cannot be invaded, penetrated or injured.

Wen Tzu adds by saying that a drunken man falls off of a cart and is not injured because he is not conscious of what is happening, is maintaining the integrity of Spirit and has no fear of dying. If you can lose the sense of self and other when drunk, imagine what truly consciously forgetting yourself can be. Enlightened human beings are identified *as*, and reside in, their Heavenly Tao-nature and are not separate from, and merge with, their surroundings and cannot be harmed.

Commentary 14 ❖ Oneness and Merging

Real attenders are:

1. Identifying *as* Original Tao; conserving, preserving and compounding Ch'i energy; are maintaining the power of

their Virtuosity, their inner Tao-nature; are uniting with natural laws and are merging with the natural order of things.[10]

2. Seeing through the differing external forms and appearances of things; are experiencing that they, and human beings engaged in the attending relationship/process, originate from the same one source of Original Tao and can merge with them; and are capable of gathering and focusing Spiritual energy and wandering and residing unharmed in that beginningless and endless Non-Being Origin where they are one with everything that comes and goes.

NARRATIVE 15
STILLNESS OF MIND

Lieh Tzu is demonstrating his archery skills to a friend. With a cup full of water balancing on his arm, he quickly let fly three arrows in a row that all hit the center of the target without spilling a drop of the water. The friend is not impressed and says to Lieh Tzu that his skill in shooting arrows is simply physical hand-eye coordination and not the state of mind characteristic of the non-shooting of a real master archer.

The friend takes Lieh Tzu up to a high mountain peak, walks to the edge of a cliff, stands backward with his heels hanging over the edge and invites Lieh Tzu to join him. Lieh Tzu falls to the ground shaking and sweating.

The friend then says that master archers can fire off arrows completely unaffected by any circumstances and under any conditions because their state of mind is constant and still. He asks Lieh Tzu to experience himself lying there on the ground in a state of anxiety having previously demonstrated his archery skills only under safe circumstances and conditions.

Commentary 15 ❖ Stillness of Mind

Real attenders are:

1. Not considering that they have mastered the art of psychotherapy when practiced under the safe conditions of, and using the coordinated skill competencies and proficiencies of, conventional psychotherapy/counseling; even when they hit the bullseye with their interpretations, interventions and interactions.
2. Experiencing that being a master psychotherapist when conducting the attending relationship/process is being in a state of mind of constant equanimity under any circumstances and conditions with any human beings, even those who are at the anxiety-ridden precipitous edges of their lives.

Narrative 16
Thinking and Doubting

Two servants of a wealthy and powerful landowner are on an errand and stay overnight at the home of an old peasant farmer. They spend the evening praising their master's wealth, power and influence and the next morning the old farmer thinks that he might make his fortune by offering his services to the landowner.

When he arrives at the landowner's mansion, he is met with a group of arrogant servants that ridicule, insult, bully and abuse him and end up tricking him into performing seemingly impossible feats for riches, i.e., jumping off a high scaffold for gold coins and diving into deep water for precious jewels. Much to the surprise of the servants, the old farmer successfully performs the feats and consequently earns their respect.

One evening, a fire breaks out in the landowner's storehouse and he offers a rich reward to anyone who can save his valuables. The old farmer immediately runs through the flames and removes all of the valuables, is admired for his courage and ability and is asked to teach the servants his apparent skills of flying through air, staying underwater and walking through fire.

But the old farmer says that he does not possess a Way or any skills, does not know how he accomplished the feats, did not even think that they were impossible or dangerous and only had his heart set on making a fortune. In retrospect and thinking about what he did; he becomes fearful, doubts his abilities and vows not to repeat his behavior even for a rich reward but still models the power of single-minded Virtuosity.

Commentary 16 ❖ Thinking and Doubting

Real attenders are:

1. Aware that for some human beings, the initial motivation for becoming a professional psychotherapist might be the single-minded prospect of accumulating wealth by conducting a high-fee thriving private practice for financially well-off patients and that they are able, in the process, to perform and successfully accomplish what appear to be impossible challenges in order to do so.
2. Fulfilling a deeply committed vocational calling; are less concerned with establishing and conducting a lucrative psychotherapy practice; and are safeguarding their Virtuosity by being more mindful, cautious and doubtful about taking on high-risk and seemingly impossible challenges for financial gain.

Narrative 17
One with Inner Nature

A ruler's animal trainer, particularly effective in taming wild animals, is retiring and the ruler sends her an apprentice to learn and continue her abilities. The animal trainer tells the apprentice that the taming of wild animals involves understanding their natural instincts and unique natures and not going against them.

The animal trainer explains that she never feeds wild animals live or whole animals so as not to arouse their ferocious killing or tearing instincts. She feeds wild animals when they just start to get hungry, and not when they are starving or full, so they will associate her with satisfying their hunger. Further, she balances both controlling wild animals and allowing them freedom so as not to provoke their anger.

Lieh Tzu says that relating to wild animals in these ways makes them feel that she is one with them and they feel at home and become tame.

Commentary 17 ❖ One with Inner Nature

Real attenders are:

1. Effective and successful in establishing safety and rapport, creating therapeutic alliances and collaborative/cooperative relationships and avoiding provoking defensive resistances, power struggles and transference acting-out with human beings by intuitively and empathically understanding and attuning to, according with and following their uniquely individual inner Tao-natures.
2. Balancing clear structure and consistent limits with allowing freedom and accepting compliance and are appropriately timing their reflections, interpretations, responses, interventions, relationships and interactions with human beings by intuitvely and empathically anticipating their receptivity and sensing their readiness.

Narrative 18
The Ferryman's Ability

After observing the gracefulness by which a ferryman handles his boat, a student consults with Confucius concerning such skill. Confucius says that it is easy for swimmers to learn to steer a boat because they understand the nature of water and that it is so natural for them to move around in it that they forget they are in the water. Underwater swimmers also learn easily because they are relaxed and not afraid of capsizing or drowning.

Confucius continues by saying that both swimmers and divers are relaxed and calm inside and are not disturbed by externals. It is like competitors in contests. When external stakes are insignificant; they are more inwardly relaxed, graceful and skillful. But when the external stakes are more significant, they can become clumsy and unskillful because they are tense and no longer relaxed and calm internally. If you become self-conscious, affected by external circumstances and lose your inner stillness, you will be clumsy and probably fail at anything you try to do.

Commentary 18 ❖ The Ferryman's Ability

Real attenders are:

1. Naturally comfortable in interpersonal relationships with human beings engaged in the attending relationship/process because they understand human nature, human being and human existence and are so familiar with relating with other human beings that they forget they are in a dualistic self-other relationship.
2. Naturally flowing and graceful in relating with human beings because they are relaxed and calm inside and not afraid of or disturbed by navigating rough waters, empathic failures, upsetting interactions, overturned interpretations, derailing interventions and possible terminations.

Narrative 19
The Swimmer's Art

Confucius and his students are standing by a steep waterfall that plummets down into a river with rushing currents so swift that it is impossible for fishes to swim in. Suddenly, they see a woman dive from the top of the waterfall into the rapids and prepare to rescue her. But the woman emerges from the waters singing. When asked about her method for surviving in such treacherous waters, she replies that she has no particular Way or method other than floating and sinking with the water and following its way instead of fighting it or trying to force her way through it.

She continues by saying that she feels safe following the natural course of living by beginning with what is given to her at birth, i.e., being born by the sea; by continuing with what is natural to do, i.e., playing in the water; and ending by trusting the destiny of what is meant to be, i.e., not thinking about how she does what she does.

Commentary 19 ❖ The Swimmer's Art

Real attenders are:

1. Diving into and riding the ups and downs of the flowing currents of interpersonal relationships with human beings and the attending relationship/process without fighting them or trying to force their way through them.
2. Safely following the natural course of their living by being consciously aware that human relationships are given to them at birth, continue as natural and enjoyable to be in and are completed by trusting and often not thinking about why or how they go as they go.

Narrative 20
Dancing with Fire

A hunting party tries to drive out animals by setting grass on fire. Suddenly, they see a man emerging from a rock and dancing in the flames and smoke. After the fires die down, they ask him about how he can come out of a rock and dance in fire. He replies that he does not know what a rock and a fire are or what they are talking about.

A student of Confucius explains that Confucius teaches that if human beings are in complete harmony and can merge with the elements, they will not be harmed by them. This is how they cannot drown in water or burn in fire. He is asked whether he or Confucius is able to do this. The student answers that he cannot and can only talk about it because he is unable to empty his mind of knowledge but that Confucius can do it but chooses not to.

COMMENTARY 20 ❖ DANCING WITH FIRE

Real attenders are:

1. Able to be in an undifferentiated, nondual, integral and empty state of pure consciousness without an object and to be in complete harmony and merge with the human beings engaged in, and the phenomena occurring in, the attending relationship/process.
2. Having no need to identify, acknowledge, dwell upon or display any of the gifts, efficacious powers and creative genius of their inner Tao-nature/Virtuosity.

NARRATIVE 21
REGULATING CH'I ENERGY

Lieh Tzu is telling his Tao-Master teacher about a clairvoyant diviner whom he believes has greater abilities than the teacher and with whom he intends to study. The Tao-Master tells Lieh Tzu that so far he has only shown him the outer surface manifestations and not the inner deeper Mysteries of Tao and asks him to bring the diviner to him for a meeting.

Lieh Tzu brings the diviner in and after the meeting is sadly told that his teacher is close to dying. Lieh Tzu reports the bad news to his teacher who tells him that he stilled Yin Ch'i vital energy in his lower/belly energy center and asks him to bring the diviner in again.

After the second meeting, Lieh Tzu is gladly told that his

teacher has already benefited from the previous meeting and is recovering. Lieh Tzu reports the good news to his teacher who tells him that this time he activated Yang Ch'i vital energy ascending from Earth in his lower/ belly energy center and asks him to bring the diviner in again.

After the third meeting, Lieh Tzu is told that his teacher is always changing and too difficult to read. Lieh Tzu reports this news to his teacher who tells him that this time he circulated alternating Yin/Yang Ch'i vital energies in the deep abysses of his middle/heart energy center and asks him to bring the diviner in yet again.

At the fourth meeting, the diviner rushes out much to Lieh Tzu's surprise who is told by his teacher that this time he showed undifferentiated primordial Ch'i vital energy descending from Heaven in his upper/head energy center and that is what frightened the diviner.

After this experience, Lieh Tzu realizes that he was seduced by power and, in reality, has not understood the very profound inner Mysteries of Tao, respectfully and humbly apologizes to the Tao-Master and returns home to live out the everyday activities of an ordinary life being free of attachments and more true to himself.

Commentary 21 ❖ Regulating Ch'i Energy

Real attenders are:

1. Able to consciously regulate and transmute vital energy/ Ch'i in their three energy centers/elixir fields/Tan T'ien and to direct and circulate it in the macrocosmic and microcosmic orbits of their bodies.
2. Not publically displaying or marketing any extraordinary psychic abilities or yogic powers and are not arrogantly taking complete responsibility for causing any of the healings and transformative changes that might be occurring in human beings during the attending relationship/process.

Narrative 22
Coming Attractions

Lieh Tzu is traveling and becomes troubled by being treated overly respectfully and given preferential treatment wherever he stops. One of his teachers shares Lieh Tzu's concern that he is doing something to invite the behavior and cautions that completely relinquishing subtle attachments to attracting such undue regard and consideration is difficult to do.

Sometime later, Lieh Tzu is visited by the teacher who turns around and leaves after seeing so many shoes in front of the doorway to his house. Lieh Tzu catches up with him and asks why he came and is leaving. The teacher replies that what he had cautioned him about earlier appears to have come true and that Lieh Tzu is still unable to prevent followers from obseqiously gathering around him because of displaying his Virtuosity.

Commentary 22 ❖ Coming Attractions

Real attenders are:

1. Not interested in amassing or colluding with a large following of dependent, submissive, deferent and obeisant human beings and are preferring to accept referrals from a limited number of professional colleagues and former and current patients who have directly experienced them.
2. Realizing that; especially when unavoidably well-enough known and genuinely well-enough respected; it is difficult to completely relinquish subtle attachments to attracting patients, students and trainees and requires intensive, extensive and ongoing self-awareness, self-reflection, self-inquiry, self-exploration, self-understanding, self-monitoring and self-regulating.

NARRATIVE 23
THE FRIENDLY DISCIPLE

Yang Chu, a disciple of Lao Tzu,[11] accompanies him on one of his sojourns and receives some surprising, puzzling and disconcerting feedback that he is unteachable, arrogant, disrespectful and consequently avoided by people. He asks for clarification and Lao Tzu explains that enlightened human beings of real Virtuosity do not regard themselves as such and are able to both transcend the ordinary everyday world and be a part of it.

Yang Chu is able to internalize, assimilate, embody, personify and enact the reality and truth of Lao Tzu's assessment and explanation as evidenced by his subsequent relaxed, friendly and enjoyable interactions with people who had previously only tolerated, distanced from and avoided him.

COMMENTARY 23 ❖ THE FRIENDLY DISCIPLE

Real attenders are:

1. Not usually friends, playmates or entertainers of human beings engaged in the attending relationship/process but are, nonetheless, warm and friendly; available, approachable and accessible and, at times, appropriately humorous, playful and enjoyable to be with.
2. Respectful of human beings engaged in the attending relationship/process and humbly grateful for, and appreciative of, the opportunity to be of inspiration, encouragement, support, assistance, guidance and benefit to them.

NARRATIVE 24
ANIMALS AND HUMAN BEINGS

Yang Chu is sojourning, stays at an inn where the innkeeper has two wives, one beautiful and one ugly, and observes that the innkeeper appears to love the ugly wife more than the beautiful one. He asks the innkeeper about this who replies that the beautiful wife thinks that she is beautiful but he does not see her beauty and the ugly wife thinks that she is ugly but he does not see her ugliness.

Yang Chu uses his experience to teach students that if human beings are true to themselves, their Virtuosity will be evident and respected. He continues by saying that external appearances cannot indicate what is inside but that human beings feel most connected with things that resemble them, e.g., some animals are as wise and caring as human beings and some human beings are as uncultivated and wild as animals. Human beings and things cannot be judged only by their external forms and appearances.

Yang Chu points out that animals behave very much like human beings, e.g., they protect and care for their young; they seek shelter and avoid danger; we can communicate with and teach them; they are good friends and companions and, in ancient times, they co-existed safely, openly and peacefully with each other and human beings.

Commentary 24 ❖ Animals and Human Beings

Real attenders are:

1. Being and living beyond the one-sidedness of socially conditioned and personally held dualistic value judgments about beings/things based upon their external appearances, e.g., being beautiful or ugly, and are experiencing that being untrue to oneself and feigning beauty can be someone's ugliness and that being true to oneself and accepting ugliness can be someone's beauty.
2. Aware of the similarities between life forms, e.g., animal instincts and human intuition; are not regarding human beings as the only sensitive, caring, intelligent, wise and cultivated beings in the universe and are not screening and selecting and assessing and evaluating human beings based upon their external appearances, characteristics and behaviors.[12]

Narrative 25
Softness and Yielding

Lieh Tzu says that in the world, strength does not always conquer and softness inevitably wins out and that yielding and non-competing free us from dangers of being defeated and worries about losing. He adds by saying that strength should be balanced with softness and that knowing when to use strength and when to be flexible, non-rigid, yielding and non-resisting has survival value.

A ruler who only surrounds himself with strong and brave men in order to feel protected is visited by a wandering philosopher who offers the ruler an alternative strategy to prevent his being injured. The philospher guides the ruler through a process of agreeing to strategies of:

1. Getting people to miss trying to injure him.
2. Getting people to not ever dare to injure him.
3. Getting people to not even wish to injure him.
4. Getting people to respect and love him.

The philosopher reminds the ruler that he already has power and of how much stronger he would be by adding Virtuosity and integrity and not more power. He points out that strength, aggression and competetiveness do not always win out; that there inevitably is someone stronger, more aggressive and competetive; and that sometimes softness, yielding and cooperativeness may be more effective.

Lao Tzu says that things that are not soft, flexible and yielding and are too hard, rigid and resistant are easily broken, accompany dying and will perish.

Commentary 25 ❖ Softness and Yielding

Real attenders are:

1. Experiencing that being soft, flexible, yielding, flowing and not resisting the resistance of human beings in

conducting the attending relationship/process are more effective in building rapport and therapeutic alliances and creating less defensiveness, resistance, reactivity, power struggles and transference acting-out.

2. Experiencing that the balancing of strong, assertive, firm and masculine Yang and soft, receptive, yielding and feminine Yin energies in their interactions and interventions synergistically increases the efficacious potency of their Virtuosity/Te.

SECTION THREE
THE NATURE OF TRANSFORMING/KING MU

INTRODUCTION

THE NARRATIVES OF SECTION THREE FOCUS ON:

1. DREAMS AND REALITY/BEING FULLY AWAKE.
2. SEEING THROUGH THE ILLUSIONS OF SELF-OTHER/SELF-WORLD.
3. FREEDOM FROM WORLDLY CONCERNS.
4. YIN/YANG CH'I/ENERGY CHANGES/IMPERMANENCE/LETTING-GO.
5. FORGETTING AND REMEMBERING.
6. EMOTIONS AND BELIEFS.
7. SELF-CREATING OF HAPPINESS/ENJOYING LIFE FULLY.
8. SPIRIT-JOURNEYING.

HUA

化

TRANSFORM/CHANGE
SMELT/MELT
DISSOLVE/EVAPORATE
YIN/YANG INTERCHANGING

PIEN

變

TRANSFORM/CHANGE
METAMORPHOSE
ALTER/BECOME
COURSE OF EVENTS

TRANSFORMING

YIN	YIN/YANG CH'I	YANG
陰	氣	陽
Shaded/dark/cloudy/cold	Animating	Sunny/bright/clear/hot
Nighttime/lunar/winter	Activating	Daytime/solar/summer
Watery/wet/soft/yielding	Complementing	Fiery/dry/firm/asserting
Inner/depth/central	Interdepending	Outer/surface/peripheral
Below/behind/within	Transforming	Above/ahead/between
Contracting/condensing	Interchanging	Expanding/radiating
Magnetic/receptive	Alternating	Dynamic/assertive
Centripetal/afferent	Reciprocating	Centrifugal/efferent
Ebbing/waning/troughing	Compensating	Flowing/waxing/cresting
Valleys/canyons/caverns	Balancing	Mountains/hills/mounds
Feminine principle in Nature	Centering	Masculine principle in Nature
Creatrix/Mother	Voiding	Creator/Father
Material Soul/P'o	reversing	Spiritual Soul/Hun

HU	HSIANG	CH'I
互	相	齊
Mutual/reciprocal	Mutual/reciprocal	Equal/equalize
Together/each other	Directed toward each other	Even/regular
Assisting/helping	Exchanging/interchanging	Together/harmonious

THE
MUTUALITY/RECIPROCITY/EQUALITY/
HARMONY OF YIN/YANG CH'I ENERGIES

Narrative 26
Spirit Journeying

A ruler is visited by a powerful sorcerer who impresses him so much that he builds palaces for him, treats him royally and provides him with the finest of earthly pleasures. But the sorcerer is not satisfied and after some time invites and transports the ruler to his own country, a heavenly realm of divine opulence far beyond the experience and imagination of the ruler. Then the sorcerer takes the ruler to another realm where lights and sounds are so intense and hellish that they disorient, overwhelm and sicken the ruler who asks for relief. In an instance, the sorcerer transports the ruler back to his palace and the ruler awakens still sitting in the same seat and in the same circumstances as before his strange experience.

After recovering, the ruler asks the sorcerer about what happened. The sorcerer tells the ruler that he went on a Spirit-journey beyond space-time and asks him whether there is any real difference between where they traveled to and where he is now. He further tells the ruler that what happened is his mind playing tricks on him and asks him who can really tell whether one situation is a reality or a dream. The ruler retires, enjoys a fulfilling life, completely transforms himself, consorts with divine and immortal beings on Sacred mountains and is believed to be a god who ascended to Heaven.

Commentary 26 ❖ Spirit Journeying

Real attenders are:

1. Realizing and experiencing that there is no real phenomenological difference between waking and dreaming life and are working with both the heavenly and hellish experiences of human beings engaged in the attending relationship/process in both realms.
2. Not necessarily prioritizing experiences of the waking life of human beings, are often working with their dreams

and may be facilitating, assisting, guiding and accompanying them on Spirit journeys to dimensions and realms of experience beyond the space-time limitations of ordinary ego-consciousness.

Narrative 27
Arcane Transforming

A wayfarer goes to learn secret mysteries from the sage Wen Tzu but starts to leave after several years of no instruction. Before his departing, Wen Tzu imparts some wisdom of his teacher Lao Tzu that all things created by the life-breath of Tao/Heaven-Earth are an illusion and that their birthing, evolving and dying are only brought about by the uniting and separating of Yin/Yang Ch'i energies. He adds by saying that the art of arcane transforming is far beyond the ordinary understanding of the superficial and illusionary changings of things and involves becoming one with the deeper creative power and transforming process of Tao and that only then can one be qualified to learn arcane arts beyond studying the illusions of body-mind.

The wayfarer returns home, diligently practices relinquishing the illusions of mind-body and after many years is able to precisely master spatial configurations, interrelationships and transformings and to realize many of the powers that transcend the ego-limitations of space-time and mind-body. He never returns to Wen Tzu or transmits his abilities to anyone else.

Lieh Tzu says that adepts and practitioners of the arcane arts do not reveal secret mysteries except to initiates after lengthy mentoring, training and practicing.

Commentary 27 ❖ Arcane Transforming

Real attenders are:

1. Understanding the transient comings and goings of transformative changes in human beings engaged in the attending relationship/process, and the process itself, as

the constantly alternating and reversing of Yin/Yang Ch'i energies that are continually uniting and creating and separating and dissolving the myriad forms of phenomenal experience.

2. Understanding that space-time, mind-body, self-other, life-death and other bipolarites of human being, existence, consciousness and experience are only transient surface illusions of the deeper mysterious creative transformings and transmutings of the Yin/Yang Ch'i energies of One/Constant Tao.

Narrative 28
Dreaming and Waking

Lieh Tzu says that waking life is characterized by eight kinds of bodily experiences, i.e., events, actions, gain, loss, happiness, sadness, life and death and that dreaming life is characterized by six kinds of mental contents, i.e., unimportant, warning, obsessive, instructive, pleasurable and frightening.

Lieh Tzu adds by saying that the rising and falling of vital energy/Ch'i in our bodies follow that of the cosmic energy/Ch'i of Heaven and Earth. Excess Yin Ch'i energy results in dreams of deep water and fears of drowning, excess Yang Ch'i energy results in dreams of hot fire and fears of burning and strong Yin/Yang Ch'i energies result in dreams of destroying or sparing life.

Lieh Tzu continues by saying that what goes on in dreaming life corresponds to, compensates for and completes what goes on in waking life. We typically dream when the mind is full, restless and attached to thoughts and we typically do not dream when the mind is empty, still and not attached to thoughts. We do not usually dream when fully awake in waking life and fully restful in sleeping life.

Lieh Tzu describes three different kinds of countries. One country receives only Yin Ch'i energies; it is mostly nightime and its inhabitants sleep most of the time, dream a lot and believe dreaming is reality. Another country receives Yin/Yang Ch'i energies equally, both night and day, and its inhabitants are awake and asleep, dream on and off and believe waking life is real and dreaming life is unreal. A third country only receives Yang Ch'i energy; it is mostly daytime and its inhabitants sleep only rarely, do not dream at all and consider it senseless to talk about dreaming and reality.

Commentary 28 ❖ Dreaming and Waking

Real attenders are:

1. Not seriously distinguishing between the phenomenological experiences of waking life and dreaming life and are being open to both as they are naturally occurring in the consciousness, awareness and experiences of human beings.
2. Assisting human beings in understanding the kinds, nature and characteristics of bodily energy experiences, emotional feelings, mental imagery and symbolic meanings of the correspondences, correlations, compensations and completions of the phenomena of both their waking and their dreaming lives.

Narrative 29
Master and Servant

A wealthy landowner, whose success is due to mercilessly exploiting his workers, fails to be compassionate toward an elderly servant who can no longer tolerate the overtaxing labors and abusive treatment and, instead, punishes him and forces him into toiling even harder and longer. During his nights, the servant dreams that he is a powerful ruler with many servants and living a life of luxury and happiness but each morning awakens to his usual miserable life. He endures suffering during the day and anticipates his enjoyable dream life at night.

Concurrently, the landowner, fatigued by managing his land

and driving his workers, sleeps a lot but his sleep is unwelcomed and restless because of recurrent nightmares that he is the indentured slave of a cruel taskmaster who forces him into long and hard labor and severely punishes him for not being productive. He cannot endure his suffering during the night, anticipates his waking life of relief from such misery and finally seeks help from a friend.

The friend points out that the dream life of the landowner is simply compensating for his waking life. The landowner realizes the misery that he is causing his servants and begins treating them humanely and compassionately. Both the miserable dreams of the landowner and the miserable life of the servant end. The servant is no longer a slave during the day and the landowner is no longer a slave at night.

Commentary 29 ❖ Master and Servant

Real attenders are:

1. Understanding the counterbalancing and compensating nature of the dreams of human beings and are assisting them in using the experiences of their dreaming life to understand and to make corresponding changes in their waking life.
2. Experiencing that when human beings are being relatively balanced selves and living generally harmonious lives, they usually are not suffering either a miserable and nightmarish waking or dreaming life.

Narrative 30
Dream and Reality

A hunter kills a deer, hides it in the forest intending to retrieve it later but, when doing so, is unable to find it and wonders whether he is dreaming that he killed a deer. He is walking back home and his questioning is shared with a man he meets who decides to try to find the deer later, does so and brings it home. After hearing the second man's story, his wife says that he finds a deer in the forest and is probably dreaming that he meets a hunter who is not sure if he really killed one or is dreaming that he did.

The hunter has returned home and is still questioning whether or not he killed a deer. That night, he dreams that he did kill a deer, hid it in the forest and sees the man he met find the deer and bring it to his own house. The next morning, the hunter goes to the man's house that he saw in his dream, finds the deer in his yard and confronts the man who refuses to relinquish the deer. A judge is called in to settle the matter but is unable to discern what is whose reality or dream and decides that the deer be equally divided between the two men.

Commentary 30 ❖ Dream and Reality

Real attenders are:

1. Experiencing that the dream experiences related to them by human beings may often have a compellingly realistic quality that makes them seem like a reality or actuality that truly occurred in their outer life.
2. Experiencing that the reality experiences reported to them by human beings may often have an unbelievably unrealistic quality that makes them seem like a dream or fantasy that fictitiously occurred in their inner life.

Narrative 31
Forgetting and Remembering

A middle-aged man completely loses his memory for how to do ordinary things and for whatever he did a moment before and is brought by family members to psychics, sorcerers, shamans and physicians who all say that they cannot help him. They finally consult with a philosopher who claims that she has a way of working on the minds of people with memory loss.

The philosopher puts the man through several initial tests that confirm his ability to appropriately react to basic needs, ascertains that he is curable and asks the family to return in seven days. No one knows the secret methods that the philosopher uses but the man is, in fact, completely cured after the seven days.

Following his recovery, the man becomes irritable and angry, acts abusively and violently toward family members, threatens the philosopher and is arrested by the police. When questioned, the man says that when he lost his memory he was content and carefree but now is plagued and overwhelmed by recalling and thinking about his past misfortunes and is certain that he will never be happy again.

Commentary 31 ❖ Forgetting and Remembering

Real attenders are:

1. Experiencing the integrative value for human beings of remembering, recollecting, reflecting upon, re-experiencing and reworking past events in their lives.
2. Aware that, for some human beings, accessing repressed and forgotten memories by remembering, thinking about, dwelling on or obsessing and ruminating about past events, may restimulate and elicit negative and upsetting emotional feelings, result in psychosomatic symptoms and provoke acting-out behavior.

Narrative 32
Mass Confusion

A father is concerned about his son's seeming confusion and interpreting and doing everything in ways opposite to conventional ones, e.g., saying black is white and acting as if wrong is right, and may be mentally ill. On the way to taking his son for help, the father meets Lao Tzu with whom he confides his concerns.

Lao Tzu questions the boy's so-called confusion, saying that many people in the world are confused and not absolutely certain about what is real or unreal, true or untrue, good or bad and right or wrong. He continues by saying that what is conventionally considered as real may only be a socially conditioned and collectively accepted consensual delusion and so who is to say who is confused, the son or the masses, and how can confused people clear up his confusion anyway?. He advises the father to forget about his son's apparent confusion and any mental illness and to return home.

Commentary 32 ❖ Mass Confusion

Real attenders are:

1. Experiencing that conventional mental conceptions of what is clear or confused, well or ill, good or bad and right or wrong are socially conditioned, collectively accepted and consensually judged and, therefore, they are staying within the uniquely subjective phenomenological frames of reference of human beings.
2. Assisting human beings in being relatively free of conventional ego-based, ego-generated, ego-derived and ego-centered socially conditioned notions concerning the nature of reality, sanity and clarity.

Narrative 33
Beliefs and Emotions

An old man is returning to his original homeland and along the way is tricked by a wayfaring companion into thinking that the first town encountered is his homeland. The companion is so convincing in pointing out landmarks, family houses, shrines and ancestral graveyards that the old man is overcome with such intense feelings of longing, nostalgia and sadness that the companion confesses to having tricked him. When the old man finally reaches his real original homeland and sees the actual landmarks, family houses, shrines and ancestral graveyards; he does not feel as sad as when he believed the trick played on him.

Lieh Tzu asks whether the old man is initially upset over nothing or whether his emotional feelings are appropriately real based upon what he really believed was true. Lieh Tzu adds by saying that human emotions have to do with internal beliefs and not necessarily with what is real or true in external reality.

Commentary 33 ❖ Beliefs and Emotions

Real attenders are:

1. Experiencing that the strong emotional attachments, real internal feelings and appropriate emotional expressions of human beings can be invoked and evoked by 'unreal', imagined and fantasized external circumstances, situations and events.
2. Often facilitating and guiding psychotherapeutic role-plays, enactments and re-enactments with human beings that activate emotional feelings, expressions, releases and catharses and that assist them in processing emotional feelings about their real-life experiences and in practicing being less emotionally attached to them.

SECTION FOUR
THE NATURE OF AWAKENING/CONFUCIUS

Introduction

The narratives of Section Four focus on:

1. Awakening/enlightened being/awareness/sageliness/ Spiritual communication.
2. Nonduality/wisdom/openheartedness/natural responding.
3. Accepting/being in tune with the natural way/course of Heaven.
4. The interconnectedness of body/mind/energy/Spirit/ surroundings.
5. Not pursuing recognition/approval/fame/fortune/ strength/power.
6. Conceptlessness/emptiness/stillness/inwardness/ naturalness/spontaneity.
7. Supporting/understanding/withdrawing/completing.
8. Letting go of the idea of happiness.

WU	MING
悟	明
Awake/aware Become conscious of/notice Apprehend/discern Intelligence Uniting Heaven-Earth in Heart-Mind	Light/bright Open/clear Evident/obvious Intelligence The brilliant light of sun/moon

AWAKENING

LIANG

亮

ENLIGHTENED
CLEAR/BRIGHT
SHINE/SHOW
ILLUMINATED/LUMINOUS
LIGHT/TRANSPARENT

MENG

夢

DREAM/DREAMING
DIM NIGHTIME VISION
HAZY/INDEFINITE
OBSCURE/CONFUSED
FANCY/PHANTASM

CHAO

昭

SHINE/SHINE FORTH
BRIGHT/BRIGHTNESS
LUMINOUS/GLORIOUS
BRILLIANT/ILLUSTRIOUS

CHAO

照

SHINE/SHINE ON
ILLUMINATE/ENLIGHTEN
LIGHT UP/REFLECT
UNDERSTAND/LOOK AFTER

THE ILLUMINATING/ENLIGHTENING CLEARNESS/BRIGHTNESS OF TAO

NARRATIVE 34
REAL HAPPINESS

Confucius retires from politics and is visited by a student who notices that his teacher appears sad and decides to leave and not intrude. Learning of Confucius's mood, another student visits happily playing a lute and singing. Confucius inquires about the happiness of the student, who says that he is carefree because of accepting life as the will of Heaven as taught to him by Confucius.

Confucius clarifies his teaching by saying that merely being happy and content with the will of Heaven is partial and that it may also sometimes bring sadness. He continues by saying that real happiness and contentment involve completely letting go of the whole idea of what it is and means to be happy and that there really is nothing about which to be either happy or sad.

COMMENTARY 34 ❖ REAL HAPPINESS

Real attenders are:

1. Experiencing the satisfaction, happiness and contentment, as well as any sadness, that accompanies acknowledging, accepting, attuning to, according with, allowing, accompanying and abiding in the will of Heavenly Tao in their meeting with human beings.
2. Understanding that completely letting go of the whole ego-based idea of what it is and means to be satisfied, happy and content opens the way to, and results in, a clearer, freer, deeper and fuller experiencing of real happiness.

NARRATIVE 35
REAL AWARENESS

Two wayfarers are meeting and sharing that they each have a sage residing in their respective countries. One man is referring to Confucius whom he says has a clear mind and an intelligent body and the other man is referring to a student of Lao Tzu whom he says can see with his ears and hear with his eyes. A ruler, hearing of the latter sage, is impressed, invites him to be his guest and inquires about his abilities.

The sage replies that he cannot see with his ears or hear with his eyes but that he can see and hear without using either. The ruler is even more impressed and inquires about this ability. The sage explains that his body is in harmony with his mind, his mind is in harmony with his energies, his energies follow his Spirit and his Spirit is attuned with Non-Being and everything around him such that nothing escapes his awareness and natural instinctual and intuitive sensing of things without his seeing or hearing.

Commentary 35 ❖ Real Awareness

Real attenders are:

1. Harmonizing their body with their mind and their mind with their vital energy/Ch'i, are following their Spirit with their vital energies and are attuned with Non-Being and their surroundings during the attending relationship/process.
2. Integrating and transcending the usual ego-separations of body, mind, self, others, world, energy and Spirit and are able to be instinctively and intuitively aware of their surrounding realities beyond the usual ego-limitations of sensory-based perception.

Narrative 36
A Real Sage

A minister is visiting Confucius and asks him if he is a sage. Confucius replies by saying that he does not claim to be one and has only read extensively and studied intensively. The minister then asks whether certain kings, emperors and lords are sages and Confucius replies that such men are wise, courageous, virtuous and timely but that he cannot say whether or not they are sages.

The minister is frustrated and asks Confucius who then does he think is a sage. Confucius says that in a far away land lives a human being who does not rule or use force and her country is peaceful and runs smoothly; who is universal, open-hearted, acts spontaneously, makes no promises and is trusted and who may be a sage but that he does not know for certain whether or not she is one.

Lieh Tzu says that it does not really matter whether or not someone is recognized as a sage as long as they are a real, true, honest and trustworthy human being.

Commentary 36 ❖ A Real Sage

Real attenders are:

1. Trusted by human beings engaged in the attending relationship/process because of conducting it open-heartedly, naturally, spontaneously, harmoniously and smoothly without managing, controlling, directing, forcing or falsely guaranteeing it.
2. Unconcerned with being recognized and identified as a wise and masterful psychotherapist/counselor and are simply being real, true, honest and trustworthy in conducting the attending relationship/process.

Narrative 37
Real Wisdom

A student is meeting with Confucius and they are reviewing some of his other students. Confucius identifies four students whom he ends up saying are, respectively more compassionate, eloquent, courageous and dignified than he himself is. The student is surprised and asks, if so, why would they want to study with him. Confucius replies by saying that the four students are also, respectively, impulsive, talkative, careless and formal and that is why they are studying with him.

Lieh Tzu says that real wisdom is not development in one or more traits but is the ability to recognize both strengths and weaknesses in ourselves and other human beings and that wise teachers, while knowing that some students may surpass them in some traits, can nonetheless assist them in developing into well balanced and well integrated human beings.

Commentary 37 ❖ Real Wisdom

Real attenders are:

1. Wisely recognizing that it is natural for human beings to possess specific characteristics, attributes, traits and qualities that both surpass and do not exceed those of their own.
2. Wisely assisting human beings in balancing and integrating their positive and negative and strong and weak characteristics, attributes, traits and qualities; in becoming a more balanced and integrated human being and in living a more harmonious life.

Narrative 38
Real Communicating

Lieh Tzu has a neighbor who appears not to recognize him whenever they see each other and, for twenty years, has never communicated with him. When a friend asks Lieh Tzu about his neighbor, he says that the man's body is still and his mind is empty, that he has transcended his senses, speaking and need for other human beings and that he is not attracted to or distracted by anything.

Nevertheless, Lieh Tzu goes to visit the neighbor along with some students. He is sitting in his house, motionless and expressionless but, to their surprise, suddenly compliments the back row of students for being deferent, impartial and inner-directed. Afterwards, the students ask Lieh Tzu what occurred. Lieh Tzu replies by saying that enlightened human beings sense the truth without reasoning, understand intent without speaking, know nothing and say nothing or very little and effectively communicate most everything Spiritually through their non-knowing and non-speaking.

Commentary 38 ❖ Real Communicating

Real attenders are:

1. Cultivating and practicing the non-knowing, non-having, non-doing and non-being of a clear mind, empty heart, still will and free Spirit in conducting the attending relationship/process.
2. Experiencing that clear, full and real communicating with human beings does not always require knowing, speaking or acting and can occur in the emptiness and stillness of silence and through intuitive sensing, indirect transmission and non-verbal body language.

Narrative 39
Real Traveling

Lieh Tzu enjoys traveling, not to see 'things' but to observe how things are changing. However, his teacher points out that he is no different from sightseers because of viewing externals and that real satisfaction is found by traveling, looking and contemplating internally.

After hearing from his teacher, Lieh Tzu stops traveling but his teacher encourages him to enjoy and perfect real traveling, to forget that he is traveling, to not know what he is looking at, to experience everything with his whole self and to make everything a part of himself by not making a distinction between himself and whatever he is seeing.

Commentary 39 ❖ Real Traveling

Real attenders are:

1. Understanding that, even though they are observing changes that are occurring in human beings engaged in the attending relationship/process and in the attending relationship/process itself, they are still objectifying external phenomena rather than experiencing their subjective internal states.
2. Forgetting the dualistic division between subject-object, seer-seen, self-other and inner-outer; are internalizing, assimilating and being one with what they are witnessing and observing in the attending relationship/process and are making it an integral part of their inner experience.

Narrative 40
Real Enlightenment

A wayfarer is conversing with a healer friend who claims to be able to cure strange illnesses. The wayfarer asks the friend if he is able to cure his strange illness which he describes as not feeling pride or disgrace when praised or blamed; not feeling happy or sad when gaining or losing; not distinguishing between fortune and misfortune, wealth and poverty, self and others, joy and sorrow or life and death; not being affected by rules, events and other people and not maintaining concern for his business, neighborhood and even family members.

The healer asks the wayfarer to face him with his back toward the sun, scans his body and tells him that his heart is empty and open and that the only thing keeping him from being a sage is his attachment to a concept of enlightenment as a strange disease.

Lieh Tzu says that there is nothing strange or mysterious about real enlightenment because it is natural and follows the natural way of things.

Commentary 40 ❖ Real Enlightenment

Real attenders are:

1. Experiencing that human beings may consider themselves to be abnormal, unwell and in need of professional help because their states of being, self-identifications and kinds of experiences do not coincide with those that are socially conditioned, conventionally regarded and consensually accepted as normal and healthy.
2. Experiencing that the real open-hearted enlightenment of human beings may seem to them to be strange and mysterious because of transcending, and not corresponding with or conforming to, conventionally agreed upon socio-cultural norms for what is natural, ordinary, normal and familiar.

Narrative 41
Real Responding

One of Yang Chu's friends dies and he attends the funeral service laughing and singing. Later, another one of Yang Chu's friends dies and, this time, he attends the funeral service weeping and sobbing.

Lieh Tzu says that Yang Chu is not being disrespectful and inappropriate in the first circumstance or inconsistent and uncontrolled in the second circumstance and is naturally expressing his real responding by celebrating the fulfilling life of the first friend and lamenting the untimely death of the second friend.

Commentary 41 ❖ Real Responding

Real attenders are:

1. Naturally, respectfully and appropriately responding to the particular differing circumstances, realities, lives and experiences of unique human beings.
2. Not attached to any fixed, consistent or conventional way

of always responding with the same feelings to similar circumstances, events and activities occurring in the experiences and lives of human beings.

Narrative 42
Real Accepting

Lieh Tzu says that when the senses begin to lose their function, they become more acute, as if struggling to sustain their effectiveness. He continues by saying that human beings, when weakening and declining, also intensify their behavior by forcing themselves to appear physically strong and mentally sharp because of not wanting to acknowledge that their lives are ending. Lieh Tzu adds by saying that enlightened human beings do not force or strain their bodies and minds, accept the natural course of things and embrace both living and dying equally.

Commentary 42 ❖ Real Accepting

Real attenders are:

1. Embracing both living and dying equally and are accepting the transient nature of their life, the life of human beings engaged in the attending relationship/process and the life of the attending relationship/process itself as the natural course of the life cycle of beginning and ending.
2. Not attempting to compensate for the ending of their life and/or the terminating of the attending relationship/process by unnaturally forcing the growing limitations of their bodies and minds beyond their naturally declining and diminishing functions and abilities.

NARRATIVE 43
REAL SUPPORT

A student of Lieh Tzu is challenged by an administrative legislator who asks him if he knows the difference between supporting oneself and being supported by others. But before the student can answer, the bureaucrat pontificates about people supported by others being like domestic animals waiting to be fed and taken care of.

The student retorts by saying that there are many wise sages, talented artists, skilled artisans and military strategists who are experts in their fields but are not good administrators and are employed by them and that untalented and unskilled bureaucrats and politicians like himself are elected and employed by citizens like him and asks the administrative legislator who then is supporting whom?

COMMENTARY 43 ❖ REAL SUPPORT

Real attenders are:

1. Highly talented, skilled and developed human beings who have expertise in conducting the attending relationship/process in creative and effective ways but who are not necessarily good administrators.
2. Generally self-supporting professionals who are self-employed in private practices and who are not usually interested in occupying official bureaucratic positions and assuming legislative administrative duties.

NARRATIVE 44
REAL STRENGTH

A man reputed to be very strong is invited by a ruler to demonstrate his strength. When the man arrives, the ruler is completely surprised by seeing a thin gangly man and questions his abilities. The man says that he is strong enough to break the wings and legs of insects. This annoys the ruler who demands to know how the man gains his reputation.

The man replies that he learned from his master teacher who was very strong but never showed his strength because he never had to use it and that he himself is learning how to gradually develop his own strength, how to not be proud of it and how to not encounter difficult situations where he would need to use it.

Commentary 44 ❖ Real Strength

Real attenders are:

1. Not needing to use physical strength in conducting the attending relationship/process or to display the psychic, transformative and healing powers that naturally accompany their personal growth, psychological development and Spiritual evolution.
2. Learning to master and avoid the difficult conditions and situations that would require or necessitate the use of strength and power and are learning how to meet ongoing challenges in conducting the attending relationship/process without forceful interventions and power struggles.

Narrative 45
Real Understanding

The highly intelligent son of a ruler who spends considerable time learning from a certain radical philosopher is questioned by a scholar who ridicules the prince's association and points out the philosopher's unorthodox, strange, eccentric and adroit way of discoursing by giving some examples of his seemingly irrational and illogical teachings. The prince defends his philosopher friend by saying that his wise teachings are used to awaken people from ignorance and are often foolishly misunderstood. He explains the undeniable and unrefutable truths of some of the paradoxical examples given by the scholar who then has nothing more to say.

Commentary 45 ❖ Real Understanding

Real attenders are:

1. Interpreting, interacting and intervening in ways that are concrete, direct and immediate and are easily, quickly and clearly understood by human beings.
2. At times, employing seemingly illogical paradoxes to assist the awakening of human beings from habitual and limiting conceptual ways of thinking about, understanding and interpreting their experiences.

Narrative 46
Real Completion

A ruler, ready to retire after fifty some years, is concerned about the success of his ruling; disguises himself as a wayfarer; travels around the country; learns that, in fact, he has been successful and retires. The sage Wen Tzu hears of this and says that whoever naturally withdraws after their work is completed understands and accords with the way of Heaven, has no conflicts with the world and allows and follows the frictionless order and effortless way of things. He adds by saying that knowing truth without attaching, being good without pretending and doing right without striving are naturally attaining, maintaining and sustaining the Way of Heaven.

Commentary 46 ❖ Real Completion

Real attenders are:

1. Knowing when the work of human beings engaged in the attending relationship/process is successfully completed and are stepping back and allowing its terminating to unfold, proceed and occur naturally.
2. Attaining, maintaining and sustaining the Tao of the attending relationship/process by being their real, true, authentic, genuine and natural selves from its initiation, throughout its duration and to and at its completion.

SECTION FIVE
THE NATURE OF UNITING/T'ANG'S QUESTIONS

Introduction

The narratives of Section Five focus on:

1. Everything originating from primordial Tao/No-Thingness/Limitlessness.
2. Everything being assisted by Heaven/following the natural order/way.
3. Oneness/Identity/dissolving subject-object separations/divisions.
4. Non-attachment/non-competetiveness/non-violence.
5. Limitedness of ordinary/everyday knowledge.
6. Non-perfecting/pushing limits/priding in accomplishments/achievements.
7. Softness/lightness over strongness/heaviness.
8. Mind-body training/balance/self-acceptance.
9. Artistry/openheartedness/the 'feel' of things/friendship.
10. Spirit-journeying.

T'UNG

同

United/together/with
Union/reunion
Share in/agreement
Similar/alike
Identical/same as

HO

合

Uniting/union
Join/pair/side by side
Bring together/combine
Agree with/conform to
Matching/equal to

THE UNITY/IDENTITY OF TAO

TAO

道

Road/path/way
Speak/guide/lead
Principle/doctrine
Ultimate Reality
Logos/Truth
Law/order/method
All That Is/As It Is
The Way

LIEN

聯

Unite/connect
Join/combine
Associate/ally with

LIEN

連

Link/connect
Join/include
Continuous/succession

HO/HE

和

United/Together with
Agreement with
Harmony/concord/peace
Join in/blend

HSIEH

協

United in/union
Be in agreement
Harmony/concord/accord
Joint/common

JOINING/CONNECTING/UNITING OF TAO-BEING

Narrative 47
Beginning and Ending

A ruler asks a sage whether things have always been here from the ancient beginning. The sage replies that they have been otherwise they would not be here now. She continues by saying that things constantly, continually and continuously come and go; that it is difficult to know when things begin and end or come before or after; that the beginning of one thing can be the ending of another and that there is no way of knowing which one comes first.

The ruler then asks if there is a finite limit or boundary to the universe. The sage replies that she does not know because No-thingness is limitless and unknowable and that there may be universes beyond this universe but that she cannot tell if there are any finite limits or boundaries within the infinite and limitless.

Commentary 47 ❖ Beginning and Ending

Real attenders are:

1. Understanding that the beginnings and endings of phenomena in the universe of human experiencing are difficult to ascertain and they are usually concerned with the birth, early life and past experiences of human beings and the constant, continual and continuous comings and goings of their current life experiences and their potential futures.
2. Experiencing that; throughout the constant, continual and continuous life course, life cycle and life span of human beings; endings are new beginnings and that the limits of, and the boundaries between, individual experiences often involve unclear interfaces and transitions.

Narrative 48
Heaven Help Us

A 90 year old man is tired of travelers having to take a long hike around two mountains to get out of the valley in which he lives, proposes that his son and grandson level the mountains blocking the way and the next day they begin chipping away at the mountains. Even though his wife tries to discourage him from such a foolish and impossible task, the old man continues digging, confident that his descendents will continue and eventually complete the work.

As it happens, mountain spirits become concerned, consult with the deities of Heaven who, seeing the old man's determination, decide to assist him and send two giants to carry away the mountains.

Commentary 48 ❖ Heaven Help Us

Real attenders are:

1. Determining that some seemingly impossible difficulties and obstructions blocking the progressing of the attending relationship/process can gradually be worked with through their constant and consistent effort.
2. Experiencing that, at times, they are being assisted by the workings of Heavenly Tao operating synchronistically and synergistically to bring about the clearing of difficulties and removing of obstructions blocking the way of progressing in the attending relationship/ process and thus opening a way through them.

Narrative 49
Deadly Pride

Lieh Tzu says that there is a great runner who so prides himself in his abilities that he decides to compete with the sun and race it across the sky to the edge of night. However, during a bright and hot day, he becomes extremely thirsty, drinks rivers dry but still dies of thirst.

Lieh Tzu says that human beings proud of their abilities often push themselves beyond their physical, mental and emotional limits and try to compete with Nature and natural events and everyone and everything around them until they inevitably lose.

Commentary 49 ❖ Deadly Pride

Real attenders are:

1. Not priding themselves in their abilities to conduct and complete the attending relationship/process efficiently and effectively beyond meeting their basic needs for self-nourishing and life-sustaining resources.
2. Understanding their abilities and shortcomings, are not competing with other professionals and are not pressuring or forcing themselves to try to perform impossible feats that exceed the normal limits of their physical, mental and emotional capacities and capabilities.

Narrative 50
The North Country

A ruler says that within Heaven-Earth and the four directions everything comes from Great Spirit and is illuminated and regulated by the sun, moon and stars and that only enlightened sages follow the natural way of things and take their place in the universe. A sage argues that there are things that exist uncreated by Great Spirit and do not require Tao and Yin/Yang Ch'i energies to illuminate and regulate them and that there are supernatural human beings who transcend the limits of space-time.

Later on, the ruler goes on a Spirit journey and travels to a country far north of his own. He discovers many strange things in this North Country, e.g., it has no boundaries, natural disasters or wild animals and in the middle of the country is a large pot-shaped mountain with a spring that flows pure, sweet, sparkling and fragrant water down the mountainside; nourishing the land, purifying the air and re-energizing the inhabitants. The people of North Country are friendly, happy and gentle; have soft bodies, clear minds and open hearts; enjoy music, singing and dancing and live healthy, long and peaceful lives. There are no rulers, regulations or conventions; no diseases, illnesses or injuries and no anxieties, fears, sorrows, pain or suffering.

Another ruler is encouraged by his advisor to visit North Country but is counseled against visiting a foreign land by his minister who reminds the ruler that his own country is beautiful and bountiful and that his subjects are cultured and peaceful. The advisor counters by saying that the minister is attached to what he has and is failing to understand the Spiritual value of keeping North Country alive and that it is ill-advised not to search for it.

Commentary 50 ❖ The North Country

Real attenders are:

1. Not believing that all human beings and the experiential phenomena of the attending relationship/process are necessarily originating from Heaven-Earth and Great Spirit or are requiring Tao and Yin/Yang Ch'i energies in order to be nourished, regulated and sustained.
2. Understanding the transformative and evolutionary value for human beings of not only being attached to their everyday lives, typical circumstances and ordinary experiences but also to keep valuing, searching for and abiding in the realities of transcendent realms, utopian ideals and transpersonal visions.

NARRATIVE 51
THE SOUTH COUNTRY

Lieh Tzu says that the people of some Southern countries have barbaric customs and practices involving bodily mutilation, human sacrifice, cannibalism and ritual cremation; the people of some Northern countries are cultured and elegant and the people of some Middle countries are conventional and modest. He adds by saying that the established customs of various countries are not barbaric or strange to the people observing and practicing them but may appear and be judged to be so by people of different countries with differing customs.

COMMENTARY 51 ❖ THE SOUTH COUNTRY

Real attenders are:

1. Accepting that human beings are all unique and different and are understanding that their racial, ethnic, national, cultural, social and familial values, customs, mores, practices and backgrounds are also unique and different and essential to be recognized and considered.
2. Not making comparative evaluative assessments or value judgments about the particular unique nature of the differing customs and practices of human beings and are accepting them with equality and impartiality, in their own right and on their own terms.

NARRATIVE 52
CHILDISH QUESTIONS

Confucius is walking through a marketplace and comes upon two children engaging in a heated argument over whether the sun is nearer or farther away when it rises or at noon judging by its size and temperature. The children ask Confucius to resolve their argument and, when he says that he is unable to tell which one of the children is correct, they both laugh saying that they thought that he is supposed to be a learned sage.

Commentary 52 ❖ Childish Questions

Real attenders are:

1. Not engaging in debates and arguments with human beings over relatively meaningless questions about the nature and realities of inexplicable phenomena.
2. Not underestimating or devaluing the real and true nature of their intelligence, insight, intuitive abilities and wisdom because they may not be appearing to be learned to human beings.

Narrative 53
Real Balancing

A fisherman using a twig for a rod, thin silk for a line, a hull of grain for a hook and a piece of rice for bait is very adept at catching large fish in spite of such fragile equipment. He is invited by a ruler to explain his art.

The fisherman says that he studied and focused on fishing for a long time and that, after some time, is able to cast a line undistracted, completely concentrating on nothing but fishing and completely contemplating nothing but fish. He continues by saying that he has a good feel for the balanced tension between the give and pull of both the water and the fishing line, that fish are not even aware of when the hook gently enters the water and that they easily swallow the natural bait.

The fisherman adds by saying that he uses what is light, soft and gentle instead of what is heavy, strong and forceful and suggests that the ruler can successfully rule the country in the same balanced way.

Commentary 53 ❖ Real Balancing

Real attenders are:

1. After much study, training and experience; completely focused and concentrated on conducting the attending relationship/process without distraction, disturbance or imbalance.

2. Using light, soft, gentle and well-balanced; rather than weighty, strong, forceful and poorly balanced; interpretations, interactions and interventions in conducting the attending relationship/process.

Narrative 54
Exchanging Problems

Two men consult the same physician about their illnesses and, in the process, she discovers that they both have more significant congenital problems affecting their hearts and minds. One man has strong ambitions and is good at planning but has weak energy and is poor at implementing and the other man has strong energy and is good at implementing but has weak ambitions and is poor at planning. The physician says that she can make them both perfect by exchanging their hearts and they both consent to the procedure.

The transplants are successful, the physician uses efficacious means to remove all signs of the surgery and the men return home but there is one major complication. The men each return to the other man's home and are not recognized by their families.

Lieh Tzu says that no one is born perfect or develops into a perfectly balanced person, that it is better to accept how one is rather than try to become someone else and that solving one relatively minor problem can create another more major one.

Commentary 54 ❖ Exchanging Problems

Real attenders are:

1. Accepting how human beings are being with respect to their unique constitutions and natures, character traits and temperments and personality characteristics and behaviors.
2. Not having treatment agendas, plans, strategies and goals to necessarily develop human beings into perfectly balanced and perfectly integrated individuals, unless that is the direction of their own intention, objective and focus.

NARRATIVE 55
THE HEART OF MUSIC

A technically proficient lute player is studying with a master musician who is able to enchant birds and fishes into dancing to her music. But after years of study, the lute player learns nothing of the art and the teacher suggests that he return home. The lute player confesses that he is unable to let music become part of himself and to play music from his heart and asks to continue practicing.

After some time passes, the master musician checks up on the lute player and, much to her delight, finds that he is able to musically evoke and interchange the qualities of each of the four seasons and to musically blend them into a beautiful, sweet, fragrant and refreshing reality.

Lieh Tzu says that the lute player, rather than only perfecting technique, is able to change reality because he is finally able to resolve the dualistic difference between himself and music, to become one with music and to play music from his heart.

COMMENTARY 55 ❖ THE HEART OF MUSIC

Real attenders are:

1. Not only technically competent and proficent in the skills and abilities involved in conducting the attending relationship/process but are doing so from their openheartedness and whole-heartedness.
2. Able to empathically attune to and to identify and unite with human beings and to allow them to become a part of themselves and the heart of their inner being and experiencing.

NARRATIVE 56
THE POWER OF SINGING

A musician decides that his study with a master singer is complete and asks to be graduated but after hearing the master sing at the graduation ceremony, so powerfully that tree leaves vibrate and clouds begin blowing, asks to be readmitted as a lifelong student.

The master singer tells him about a woman in need of money who sings at a local tavern one evening and the sound of her voice remains in the tavern for days. Later she stays at an inn and one evening, when she sings a sad song, her voice carries throughout the town causing the townsfolk to weep. And the following day, when she sings a joyful song, they laugh and dance. The townsfolk learn to sing like the woman and, after she leaves, the town becomes well known for its powerfully evocative singers.

COMMENTARY 56 ❖ THE POWER OF SINGING

Real attenders are:

1. Aware that the level, degree and extent of their mastery of the talents and abilities involved in conducting the attending relationship/process are never complete and can always be further developed.
2. Models for human beings and are naturally inspiring and stimulating them in evoking, developing and expressing their own unique gifts, talents, Virtuosity and potentials.

NARRATIVE 57
ONENESS IN MUSIC

Two good friends are one in music. One is a fine lute player and the other a fine listener and she can feel the identical mood with vivid imagery of whatever the lute player has on his mind when he plays, e.g., misty rains, lofty mountains, flowing waters.

The lute player is ecstatic over having his mind and heart read and joined by his good friend.

Lieh Tzu says that the two friends are kindred spirits who dissolve the barriers that separate them from each other and that the music is a bridging vehicle that allows them to connect and to commune with each other in their hearts and minds.

Commentary 57 ❖ Oneness in Music

Real attenders are:

1. Acknowledging being unique and different individuals from other human beings but who are also able to bridge separateness and to inwardly experience their inner feelings through active listening, intuitive sensing, empathic attuning and harmonic resonating.
2. Not attached to being separate and different from other human beings and are able to find them inside of themselves and to intersubjectively join, connect, identify, unite and merge with them within the oneness of the context and medium of the attending relationship/process.

Narrative 58
Artificial Reality

A ruler inquires about the skills of a craftsperson who claims to be able to make anything for which he is commissioned. The craftsperson demonstrates his skills by bringing his latest creation to the ruler, which appears to be a man who is able to talk, sing and dance. The ruler is amazed that the 'man' looks and acts so much like a real person that he arranges a performance and invites his favorite female attendants to attend.

However, at one point during the performance, the artificial 'man' casts a flirtatious glance at one of the women. The ruler is outraged and threatens to execute the craftsperson who quickly disassembles the artificial man to prove that he is not a real person. Now, the ruler is really amazed that the skills of the craftsperson can model a human being created by Heaven-Earth.

Lieh Tzu asks if there is any difference between real and artificial, since human beings are no more special than other natural creations and since both human beings and the 'man' are composed of natural materials created by the same one primordial Ch'i energy of Tao and the uniting of Yin/Yang Ch'i energies.

Commentary 58 ❖ Artificial Reality

Real attenders are:

1. Not making hard and fast distinctions between what is real and artificial in conducting the attending relationship/process and, at times, may craft role plays, re-enactments and psychodramas that result in real awakenings and transformative experiences for human beings.
2. Appreciating that regardless of whether the experiences occurring in the attending relationship/process are considered as real or artificial, they both are sourced in the Non-Being of Tao and are created by the dynamic operating of Yin/Yang Ch'i energies.

Narrative 59
Friendly Rivals

A wayfarer desires to apprentice with a master archer and to learn, and possibly exceed, his skills. The master archer requires that the apprentice first train his eyes to not blink under any conditions, to enlargen small objects and to clear blurry images and, after years of successful practicing, finally accepts him.

The wayfarer's archery skills become highly developed and are only exceeded by those of the master teacher whom he plans to kill in order to be the greatest archer. One day, the two happen to meet and the wayfarer immediately sends off a number of arrows toward his former teacher who quickly counters each of them in midair with his own arrows and, having run out of arrows, counters the last arrow of the wayfarer with a stick.

Both men drop their bows, bow to each other, pledge to be as father and son and vow never to teach their skills to others, lest they become used as a matter of jealousy and treachery.

Commentary 59 ❖ Friendly Rivals

Real attenders are:

1. Not jealous or envious of teachers, trainers, mentors or master psychotherapists/ counselors and are free of needs to compete with them or to exceed their proficiency.
2. Not jealous or envious of students, trainees or human beings engaged in the attending relationship/process who may rival or exceed their own talents and abilities and are continuing to serve, support, assist, facilitate and guide them in their self-developing and self-mastery.

Narrative 60
Mind-Body Training

A wayfarer apprentices himself to a master charioteer. After several years, the master begins to instruct the apprentice in a way to achieve the state of body and mind that he is in when driving a chariot. The instruction involves training the apprentice's body and hands to respond to the directions of his mind so that he is able to physically apply and release pressure in the reins and to effortlessly transfer his mental intentions to the horses.

The master further instructs that the reverse happens and that the horses' movements are transferred through the bit and bridle to the reins and to his hands, the rest of his body and his mind and that precise control of the horses occurs through intention, communication, feedback and feel.

Lieh Tzu says that intentions are communicated most naturally when our body is relaxed and flexible and our mind is clear and still and both are working simultaneously and cooperatively.

Commentary 60 ❖ Mind-Body Training

Real attenders are:

1. Experiencing the importance of conducting the attending relationship/process with a relaxed and flexible body and a still and clear mind in order to naturally empathize, interact and communicate with human beings.
2. Experiencing that their intentions and those of human beings are mutually communicated through the interconnectedness and resonances of their respective minds and bodies, feedback loops and intuitive 'feel'.

Narrative 61
The Magical Sword

A wayfarer vows to avenge his father's death by killing his murderer but is at a loss because of the fraility and weakness of his body. A friend knows of a nobleman who has very powerful swords that nonetheless can be wielded by a child and suggests that the wayfarer see if he can borrow one.

The wayfarer visits the nobleman who sympathizes with him and says that he has three magical swords but none of which will kill anybody or cause bleeding. One cuts invisibly, another cuts painlessly and a third inflicts slight pain. The wayfarer chooses the third sword, finds his father's murderer drunk at home, slashes him from neck to waist and, on his way out, also slashes the arms and legs of the man's son who asks him why he is there and waving his arms in such a peculiar way.

Later on, the murderer complains of a sore throat and painful waist and his son complains of aching arms and legs. The son asks why the wayfarer ran out of their house waving his arms and they wonder if he had cursed them.

Lieh Tzu says that, at least, the wayfarer took matters into his own hands, expressed his anger and avenged his father's death by not killing his murderer, provoking the son's revenge against him and his family and perpetuating vendettas.

Commentary 61 ❖ The Magical Sword

Real attenders are:

1. Fundamentally non-aggressive, non-invasive and non-violent and are not conducting the attending relationship/process in ways that might be unintentionally or inadvertantly painful for, or rewounding of, human beings.
2. Assisting human beings in dealing with anger, grief and revenge through empowering role-playing and expressive re-enactments that allow them to experience and release emotional feelings without perpetuating cycles of violence and revenge in their lives.

SECTION SIX
THE NATURE OF FOLLOWING/DESTINY

INTRODUCTION

THE NARRATIVES OF SECTION SIX FOCUS ON:

1. DESTINY/LUCK/TRUST/CHANGES NATURALLY COMING ABOUT BY THEMSELVES BEYOND CONTROL.
2. ACCEPTING/ALLOWING THE NATURAL ORDER/FLOW/COMINGS AND GOINGS/UNFOLDING OF EVENTS.
3. LETTING THINGS GO ACCORDING TO THEIR NATURAL COURSE/NOT EFFORT/FORCING/INTERFERING.
4. CYCLES OF TRANSFORMING/ONE THING FOLLOWS ANOTHER/MAY TURN INTO ITS OPPOSITE.
5. NOT TRYING TO MAKE THINGS HAPPEN OR TO PREVENT THEM FROM HAPPENING.
6. NON-ATTACHMENT TO PAST-PRESENT/SUCCESS-FAILURE/FORTUNE-MISFORTUNE/LIVING-DYING.
7. INDIVIDUAL DIFFERENCES/NATURAL DISPOSITIONS/INDIVIDUAL PATHS.
8. REAL FRIENDSHIP/NOT SOCIALLY CONDITIONED ILLUSIONS OF WORTHINESS.

TS'UNG

从 從

FOLLOWING
COMPLYING WITH/OBEYING
JOINING/ENGAGING IN
AGREEING WITH

SUI

隨

FOLLOW
ACCORD/COMPLY WITH
ACCOMPANY/ALLOW
RESEMBLE/LOOK LIKE
LET DO AS ONE LIKES

I

依

FOLLOW
AGREE/COMPLY WITH
RELY ON/DEPEND ON
ACCEDE/CONFORM TO
TRUST TO

ACCORDING/ALLOWING/ FOLLOWING/ACCOMPANYING

WU WU WEI CH'I WEI

WU	WU WEI CH'I	WEI
無	氣	爲
No-/not/non-/un- Without Nothing/no-'thing'	Tao-Sourcing Flowing Circulating Rotating Revolving Cycling Returning	Do/act/make/cause Act as/serve as Practice/cultivate

MING	T'ING	LIU
命	聽	流
Destiny/fate Life/life span	Allow/let Comply/obey	Flow/current Circulate/spread

NON-DOING/THE LETTING OF/ ALLOWING OF/ COMPLYING WITH THE FLOWING/CIRCULATING/ RETURNING DESTINY OF TAO

Narrative 62
Effort and Destiny

Lieh Tzu says that some things can be accomplished through human effort but that many events are beyond human control and effort, come about by themselves and are a matter of destiny. He points out paradoxes that intelligent, virtuous, honorable, hard-working, capable and beneficent human beings can be poor and destitute and die ignoble, violent and early deaths and that unintelligent, unvirtuous, corrupt, indolent, inept and harmful human beings can be wealthy and prosperous and live famous, peaceful and long lives.

Lieh Tzu continues by saying that benefit may later turn into harm and harm may later turn into benefit and advises allowing events to naturally come about and unfold of themselves without trying to either promote or prevent them and without being attached to either fortunate and successful or unfortunate and unsuccessful outcomes and results.

Commentary 62 ❖ Effort and Destiny

Real attenders are:

1. Experiencing that, while many successful and fortunate outcomes of the attending relationship/process come about through their conscious efforts and those of human beings; many others appear to be the result of factors, circumstances and events beyond their control and efforts with no inherent guarantee of either succeeding or failing.
2. Understanding that many of their successful interpretations, interactions and interventions are a matter of unpredictable and serendipitous happenings and optimal timeliness and fortunate opportunities and they are not necessarily trying to prevent experiences from occurring or to be attached to their outcomes.

Narrative 63
For What It's Worth

Two old friends who grew up together, but who have not kept up their friendship, are reviewing some of their life experiences. It turns out that their lives have been very different in spite of their common backgrounds. One friend is fortunate, successful, recognized, respected, welcomed, attended to, trusted and promoted and the other friend is unfortunate, unsuccessful, unrecognized, disrespected, avoided, ignored, distrusted and dismissed.

The unfortunate friend asks the fortunate friend if he considers himself more worthy who then says that he does not know who is more worthy but that things go right for him rather than wrong and that, consequently, he may be regarded as more worthy. The unfortunate friend is hurt, departs and comes across a sage who is concerned about his obviously feeling shame and accompanies him back to the more fortunate friend to repair the insult.

The sage points out how the unfortunate friend has more worth but less luck and feels ashamed and the fortunate friend has more luck but less worth and feels presumptuous and that they both are forgetting that worthiness and unworthiness are both Heaven-given just as they are. He adds that both friends are blinded by their illusions and interpretations of worthiness based upon societal norms.

In this single meeting, the seemingly unfortunate friend is enlightened and able to fully accept and contentedly enjoy his life just as it is without knowing anything about, or comparing, worthiness and unworthiness.

Commentary 63 ❖ For What It's Worth

Real attenders are:

1. Not priding in positive qualities, worthy virtues, social status, successful accomplishments and professional reputation; which they feel are mostly beyond their control and a matter of the good fortune and luck of their

endowment (en-Tao-ment) by Heavenly Tao.

2. Experiencing that their value and worth as human beings are not based upon, or measured by, conventional social norms of how much they are knowing, having, doing and being and they are, rather, gratefully accepting, fully living and contentedly enjoying their life just *as* it is.

Narrative 64
Coincidental Unfolding

Two best friends are both advisors to two different rulers who, during a time of great political upheaval, become vicious enemies battling for power and control. The advisor to the winning ruler is appointed as a minister, indicates that it is time to build the country and suggests that his best friend be given a ranking position. Overcoming the fact that the best friend originally is an enemy, the ruler is so impressed by him that he appoints him as a higher ranking chief minister who quickly becomes the second most powerful statesman next to the ruler.

Out of mutual respect, the first best friend is not resentful about initially being outranked by his friend or jealous of his success and continues their friendship even subsequently when the friend recommends someone other than himself to be his successor whom he finds to be more suitable.

Lieh Tzu says that both friends are objective and realistic in their evaluations of each other's qualities and abilities and do not have personal ambitions or show personal favoritism over the needs and welfare of the country and that coincidence and the alternating of favor and disfavor play a determining role in the inevitable unfolding of events in their lives.

Commentary 64 ❖ Coincidental Unfolding

Real attenders are:

1. Not personally ego-invested in, or ego-attached to,

meeting their own needs over against serving, encouraging, supporting, assisting, facilitating and guiding human beings in actualizing their potentials, accomplishing their objectives, being themselves and living their lives.

2. Offering feedback to human beings that is objective, realistic and appropriate and not falsely positive based upon personal preferences, misperceptions, projections, selective reinforcement, inauthentic support or favoritism.

Narrative 65
Cycles of Transforming

A prominent government official who delights in fault-finding and conflict-stirring criticizes a minister's adopting of stringent regulations and strict enforcements. The minister becomes angry over his disturbing, disruptive and divisive assertions and has him arrested and executed.

Lieh Tzu asks whether the minister needed to have the offical killed to prevent internal disorder and also whether the official needed to oppose the minister and invite trouble for himself. He continues by saying that the circumstances could not have unfolded and been completed otherwise and that both the minister and the official have no other choice given the nature of the circumstances and their natural dispositions.

Lieh Tzu adds by saying that in the natural order of things, the timeliness of our life and death is not absolutely controllable by us and occurs in the context of, and through the convergence of, multiple factors and that the cycles of transforming of Heaven-Earth are a matter of the unchangeable natural order and comings and goings of things that need to be recognized and accepted as such silently, harmoniously and peacefully.

Commentary 65 ❖ Cycles of Transforming

Real attenders are:

1. Experiencing that playing the devil's advocate, opposing and arguing with human beings engaged in the attending relationship/process do not result in its effective conduct and successful progress and are usually experienced as empathic failures that ignore their uniquely natural dispositions and result in power struggles, derailed process, acting-out and early termination.
2. Quietly, harmoniously and peacefully accepting that they are not absolutely or completely in control of the natural unfolding, inevitable course, ultimate destiny and final outcome of the attending relationship/process which may be more a matter of the convergence of natural dispositions and a multiplicity of situational and circumstantial factors and variables.

Narrative 66
No Treatment Needed

Yang Chu's friend becomes ill and refuses treatment which upsets his sons who start to mourn his worsening condition. Yang Chu visits his friend, is invited by him to sing a song that will awaken the sons and sings about unknowing, the futility of crying and the healing limitations of physicians and shamans. The song does not help the sons to understand and they invite three physicians to examine their father.

The first physician diagnoses an imbalance in Yin/Yang Ch'i energies; recommends proper eating and sleeping, abstinence, less worry and more rest and is dismissed by the father as being of average ability. A second physician diagnoses prenatal deficiencies and a congenitally weak constitution; indicates that there is little that can be done at this late date and is regarded by the father as being of good ability. The third physician does not even examine the father and says that his illness is not caused by Heaven-Earth, human beings or evil spirits; that the life course cannot be controlled or directed and that no treatment is necessary. The father is pleased with the third physician and rewards his competency. Shortly thereafter, the father recovers naturally.

Lieh Tzu says that overvaluing life and overattaching to health invite and risk losing both and that living and dying and health and illness come of themselves and advises to let things go according to their natural course without trying to make things happen or to keep them from occurring.

Commentary 66 ❖ No Treatment Needed

Real attenders are:

1. Of average ability when considering the symptoms of illness as an imbalance in vital energies that can often be corrected with proper diet and rest, abstinence and decreased worry and are of good ability when recognizing the prenatal, congenital and constitutional foundations of illness that are often refractory to treatment.
2. Experiencing that, at times, it is unecessary to treat what may appear to human beings to be illness and to accept the state of health as a matter of the natural course and cycle of living and dying and to be open to spontaneous remission and natural healing to occur.

Narrative 67
Trusting and Destiny

Lao Tzu instructs his student Wen Tzu that ungifted human beings are not necessarily unfavored by Heaven and that there is no necessary relationship between grace, talent and ability and well or ill-being because no one knows the will of Heaven and it may be that being or seeming unblessed is assisting them.

Yang Chu's brother asks him about some things that he does

not understand, e.g., when two men are endowed with the same gifts at birth and are of equal age, intelligence, appearance and demeanor; why is one favored, healthy, wealthy and respected and the other is unfavored, ill, poor and disrespected.

Yang Chu explains that the differing life course of the two men is a matter of the laws of Heaven-Earth, the natural unfolding of events or destiny, and is not determined solely by their innate ability or conscious effort. He continues by saying that trusting and accepting the natural order and course of things free us from worries about the length of our life, the state of our health and what is right or wrong and that trusting in and being true to ourself free us from being affected or disturbed by the happenings of our life, e.g., gain-loss, approval-disapproval, praise-blame, happiness-sadness, anger-contentment.

Yang Chu adds by saying that enlightened human beings do not question why or how they are living, are not affected by the opinions of others, are not going against their own inner nature or the natural grains of things, are coming and going alone and are accepting the natural unfolding and course of things.

Commentary 67 ❖ Trusting and Destiny

Real attenders are:

1. Acknowledging and accepting that there is no necessary relationship between the endowed talents, acquired abilities and exerted efforts of human beings and their health, well-being, success and longevity and that they may have difficulty understanding and be disturbed by this reality, especially when their lives are not going according to their expectations.
2. Acknowledging, accepting and not questioning the natural order, course and unfolding of experiences in their lives and those of human beings, many of which are fundamentally beyond their control, and are encouraging them to trust in and be true to themselves and to not be affected by external circumstances and the opinions of others.

Narrative 68
Individual Differences

Five separate groups of four people each are living together and each member of each group is very different from the others in personality traits, dispositions, interests and behaviors which results in comparisons, misunderstandings, judgments and conflicts. Each individual in each group believes themselves to be more intelligent, gifted, virtuous, skillful and resourceful.

Lieh Tzu says that all of these people do things in their own way; appear to have little or no interest in learning, knowing about or understanding each other and could be considered snobbish and anti-social. He continues by questioning whether they can be successful in understanding each other and says that the individuals are all different from each other and following their own path in life, that it is more honest to accept and trust individual differences in destinies than to politely pretend interest or feign understanding and that it is a rare blessing and gift when individuals can communicate truly and directly and commune intimately and wholeheartedly.

Commentary 68 ❖ Individual Differences

Real attenders are:

1. Recognizing that human beings are absolutely unique and different individuals and are encouraging, supporting, assisting, facilitating and guiding them to realize and actualize their unique personality traits, dispositions, interests, behaviors and activities and to discover and follow their own life-paths without comparing, evaluating and judging themselves in relation to other human beings.
2. Interested in accepting, appreciating and valuing the realities and actualities of individual human beings as they are; are offering feedback directly, concretely, honestly and non-judgmentally without feigning interest or understanding and are considering it a blessed gift and precious opportunity to be meeting intimately and wholeheartedly with them in the attending relationship/process.

Narrative 69
Succeeding and Failing

Lieh Tzu says that we often do not know ahead of time whether we will succeed or fail in our endeavors, so why waste time and energy trying to anticipate outcomes and be anxious and apprehensive. He adds by saying that many things happen by destiny without our active intervening and that when we accept the natural flowing of events we are more emotionally stable and unreactive.

Lieh Tzu continues by saying that living and dying are natural, wealth and poverty are circumstantial and praise and blame are interpersonal, so why worry about whether life is long or short or we succeed or fail or we are accepted or rejected, since events come and go of themselves and our worrying does not change them. He adds by saying that intelligent human beings try to calculate the probability of events occurring but that they turn out the way they do independent of predictions. Lieh Tzu concludes by saying that when we do not anticipate or expect either success or failure, we are ready to naturally accept any outcome or result with equanimity.

Commentary 69 ❖ Succeeding and Failing

Real attenders are:

1. Efficiently and effectively conducting the attending relationship/process without anticipating, calculating, expecting or predicting the probability of its succeeding or failing and are allowing and accepting the way in which it is naturally unfolding, proceeding, developing, progressing and completing.
2. Sustaining their equanimity regardless of how successfully or unsuccessfully the attending relationship/process is unfolding and proceeding without actively interfering with it through specific interpretations, interactions and interventions that are designed to bring about their own desired aims and objectives or outcomes and results.

NARRATIVE 70
ATTACHING TO LIVING

A ruler, traveling throughout his country and surveying its beauty, is deeply saddened by the prospect of dying and leaving it. Two officials start to weep with him but the chief minister chuckles to himself and is asked by the ruler to explain his amusement. The chief minister replies that if everyone lived forever, ancient rulers would still be ruling and he, the current ruler, would likely be a peasant plowing fields somewhere else, toiling to make a living and contemplating the relief of dying. The ruler understands his lineage and apologizes for his emotions and for not setting a good example for his officials.

Lieh Tzu says that when we are wealthy, famous and powerful, we may not want to die and, when we are poor, toiling and suffering, we may want to die and that both are only momentary wishes. He continues by saying that joy or misery do not last forever, that fortune and misfortune come and go in their own way, that we should not either attach to living or desire dying and that both come on their own at their own time, so why want living and fear dying?.

COMMENTARY 70 ❖ ATTACHING TO LIVING

Real attenders are:

1. Appreciating and enjoying their present living and the lives of human beings just as they are; are realizing the transiency of living and the inevitability of dying and are generally unconcerned , unworried and unanxious about, unattached to and unfearful of when the ending of their lives or the termination of the attending relationship/process will occur.
2. Using any concerns, anxiety, sadness and fears about dying and the ending of their living as stimuli, catalysts and models for potentiating and committing to living life as consciously and fully as possible in order to prevent experiencing the losses and regrets of an unfulfilled life when it ends.

NARRATIVE 71
THEN AND NOW

A man's only son dies of a sudden illness and he is not saddened or mournful. His wife is puzzled, curious and inquires about his behavior feeling that he loved their son and should be heartbroken instead of acting as if nothing has happened. The man replies that before his son was born, he had no son and was not heartbroken and now that he has no son again, why should he be heartbroken?.

COMMENTARY 71 ❖ THEN AND NOW

Real attenders are:

1. Valuing, appreciating and enjoying living the present-time of their lives and are being grateful for its blessed gift, precious treasure and great opportunity; knowing full well that its ending could occur at any moment.
2. Accepting birthing as the changing of all that came before the present-time of their lives and dying as the changing of all that comes after the present-time of their lives and are understanding that birthing and dying ultimately are not the gaining or the losing of life.

SECTION SEVEN
THE NATURE OF ENJOYING/YANG CHU

INTRODUCTION

THE NARRATIVES OF SECTION SEVEN FOCUS ON:

1. SEEING THROUGH THE ENSLAVING ILLUSIONS OF STATUS/WEALTH/FAME/LONGEVITY/IMMORTALITY.
2. THE EMPTINESS/MEANINGLESSNESS/NOTHINGNESS OF RECOGNITION/HONORS/TITLES/REPUTATION.
3. LETTING LIFE/DEATH RUN THEIR NATURAL COURSE/NOT GOING AGAINST THE NATURAL ORDER OF THINGS.
4. BEING TRUE TO ONESELF/NOT RESTRAINING/ GOING AGAINST ONE'S NATURE/NATURAL INSTINCTS.
5. NOT SACRIFICING/LOSING HEALTH/WELL-BEING/INTEGRITY/HUMILITY/FREEDOM/HAPPINESS/'HEART'.
6. KNOWING WHEN TO STOP/WHEN ENOUGH IS ENOUGH/BEING SUFFICIENT/NOT OVERWORKING.
7. NOT WASTING TRANSIENT LIFETIME ON SMALL/TRIVIAL MATTERS OR TRYING TO MAKE A DIFFERENCE.
8. CULTIVATING LIVING SIMPLY/FREELY/CONTENTEDLY/HAPPILY/PLEASURABLY/ENJOYABLY/OPTIMALLY.
9. NOT LIVING LIFE IN TERMS OF THE NEEDS/WANTS/DESIRES/WISHES/DEMANDS OF OTHER PEOPLE.
10. MAKING OPTIMAL USE OF/THE BEST OF AND ENJOYING THIS SHORT/TRANSIENT/IMPERMANENT LIFE.

HSIANG

享

ENJOY
RECEIVE/ACCEPT
PRESENT/OFFER UP
A GIFT/SACRIFICE

SHANG

賞

ENJOY
APPRECIATE
BESTOW/GRANT
AWARD/REWARD

ENJOYING

TZU		JAN
自		然
Self/oneself I/me/my Of course Certainly	Presence Spontaneity Freedom Nature	So/thus Like this Yes/right/correct Still/nevertheless

LE/LO	HSI
樂	喜
Happiness/Joyfulness Gladness/Cheerfulness Pleasure/Laughter Music	Happiness/Joy Gladness/Delight in Pleasure/Enjoyment Singing/Drumming

THE NATURAL SPONTANEOUS PRESENCING/JOYOUS HAPPINESS OF EXPERIENCING/BEING TAO

Narrative 72
Freedom and Happiness

Yang Chu is traveling and stays with a friend who asks him why people are not satisfied with who they are and seek social recognition. Yang Chu replies by saying that such recognition makes people wealthy, wealth makes them powerful, power makes them secure before they die and security enables them to provide for their descendents. The friend then asks how a reputation can affect the welfare of descendents.

Yang Chu explains that people think that a good reputation is passed on to descendents but that honesty and humility do not necessarily result in power and rank and that wealth and power often involve sacrificing honesty and humility. He adds by saying that name, power and fame are nothing, empty and meaningless; that reputation necessarily does nothing to benefit descendents and that people without social recognition, status and reputation to uphold are freer and happier.

Commentary 72 ❖ Freedom and Happiness

Real attenders are:

1. Satisfied in their professional practice and are not sacrificing their integrity by being motivated to attain social recognition, monetary wealth, personal power, famous reputation or inheritable assests.
2. Freely committed to, and happily fulfilled by, being humble, honest and virtuous human beings in their lives and in professionally conducting the attending relationship/process.

Narrative 73
Enjoying the Sojourn

Yang Chu says that living one-hundred years is not really living long, e.g., half of the time is spent in childhood, sleeping and old age; much life time is sacrificed, wasted and lost in illness, sadness, anxiety, confusion, overworking, pain and suffering and little precious life time is left to be free and to enjoy life. He adds by saying that people are enslaved and imprisoned by striving for, pursuing and attaining social recognition, personal satisfaction, self-fulfillment and gainful achievement at the expense of their hearts.

Yang Chu continues by saying that human life is a temporary sojourn in this world and death is a temporary departure from it and that we should listen to our inner voice, freely live and fully enjoy a life of our own, follow our hearts guided by the natural order of things and not live a life of meeting other people's demands, following their rules, pleasing them and/or being manipulated by them in order to achieve the burdens of fame and recognition.

Commentary 73 ❖ Enjoying the Sojourn

Real attenders are:

1. Living their lives, regulating their vital energies and conducting the attending relationship/ process economically and efficiently without sacrificing and wasting precious life time in non-essential, irrelevant, meaningless, useless and pointless thoughts, feelings, behaviors, activities and interactions.
2. Appreciating human living as a temporary sojourn and are making optimal use of their lives by following their inner truth; not sacrificing their heart, freedom and enjoyment; serving, contributing to and benefiting human beings and not being enslaved and imprisoned by seeking, pursuing and attaining social recognition and famous reputation through conformity to conventions and manipulation by others.

NARRATIVE 74
THE INEVITABLE EQUALIZING

Yang Chu says that, in life, human beings are different in many ways but, in death, are the same and that our human living and dying are beyond our control, come and go of themselves and are matters of destiny. He continues by saying that, regardless of who we are, we all die and that, given the shortness of our transient human life, we should make the best of it and enjoy it while we can.

COMMENTARY 74 ❖ THE INEVITABLE EQUALIZING

Real attenders are:

1. Realizing that their human living, the living of human beings and the life of the attending relationship/process are all transient and will, at some point, end in a death and termination that may be beyond their control and come and go according to the nature of the human life course and life cycle.
2. Appreciating the blessed gift and precious opportunity of human living, are making optimal use of it and are enjoying it as much as possible.

NARRATIVE 75
POVERTY AND WEALTH

Yang Chu says that both poverty and wealth can hurt us because both involve needing to toil to either make or to keep money and that the best way to live is contentedly with sufficient means to adequately enjoy life and to avoid the extremes of being either too poor and impoverished by necessities or too wealthy and burdened by responsibilities.

Commentary 75 ❖ Poverty and Wealth

Real attenders are:

1. Striking a happy medium and living a middle way between the extremes of not being either too poor or too wealthy but having enough means to sufficiently support and adequately enjoy their living.
2. Stopping and accepting when they have enough means to live a sufficient, adequate and contented life and are not toiling to either make and have enough money or to keep and make more money.

Narrative 76
Cultivating Living

Yang Chu says that two wayfarers are discussing what cultivating living is and what handling dying is, the way to live and to die.

One wayfarer says that cultivating living is naturally taking care of ourselves and living freely without restricting, constraining or injuring ourselves by denying our wills or by conforming to who others want us to be or complying with what they want us to do.

The other wayfarer says that handling dying is simply accepting when our death comes and not worrying about what happens after we die.

Yang Chu says that between the two wayfarers, they cover the way to live contentedly and sufficiently and the way to die simply and freely.

Commentary 76 ❖ Cultivating Living

Real attenders are:

1. Cultivating living by freely, sufficiently and contentedly being who they naturally are and not being defined and determined by, or necessarily conforming to and complying

with, the wants and demands of other human beings.

2. Handling dying by simply accepting that living and dying continually come and go and that their dying and the termination of the attending relationship/process will naturally come when they come.

Narrative 77
Insane or Enlightened?

A very wealthy man is living an extravagant life of opulence, luxury and indulgence but also is extremely generous and philanthropic. Near the ending of his life, he gives away all of his treasured possessions, leaves no inheritance for his family and becomes so poor that there is no money to pay for his medical and eventual funeral expenses.

A scholar hearing of the man calls him an insane person who squanders his wealth, abandons his family and disgraces his ancestors. A philosopher hearing of the man counters by calling him an enlightened person who is not constrained by social conventions, follows his heart, does not go against his nature, enjoys himself and gives freely.

Lieh Tzu asks us to decide whether the man is insane or enlightened.

Commentary 77 ❖ Insane or Enlightened?

Real attenders are:

1. Integrating, supporting and enhancing their own lives freely and enjoyably and contributing and donating to the lives of human beings freely and generously.
2. Experiencing that, at times, it may be difficult to definitively ascertain whether human beings are insane or enlightened when they appear to either ignore or to transcend consensus realities, social conventions and normative expectations.

Narrative 78
Pleasure and Work

A minister has two brothers both of whom appear to be lost in the sensory indulgences of unconscious, irresponsible and debased life styles. He consults with a fellow statesperson about his concerns and follows his suggestion to tell the brothers about the need to take care of their health, control their passions, order their lives and act responsibly.

The brothers say that they are aware of the dangers of their lifestyles; that life is precious and short; that they want to enjoy it; that the minister also is damaging his own health and endangering his own life by suppressing his natural instincts, doing the bidding of others and toiling so hard and that they are being more true to themselves and honest with others.

Commentary 78 ❖ Pleasure and Work

Real attenders are:

1. Maintaining a healthy balance between acknowledging their natural instincts and fulfilling their cultural intelligence and are being true to their inner nature and honest in relation to human beings engaged in the attending relationship/process.
2. Not denying, repressing or suppressing their instinctual nature; not depleting their vital energy by overworking; and not engaging in the politics of psychotherapy/counseling.

Narrative 79
Longevity and Immortality

Yang Chu is asked what he thinks about people who pray for longevity and immortality. He replies that dying is beyond our control, that everyone dies sometime and that praying will not help. Yang Chu continues by asking why do we want to live long or forever and go through the same things happening. He also says that suicide is not an alternative either and that we should just accept life, allow it to run its natural course and go to death peacefully. Yang Chu adds by saying that life and death come by themselves and we should not try to delay or accelerate either one of them.

Commentary 79 ❖ Longevity and Immortality

Real attenders are:

1. Comfortably and peacefully accepting the natural progressing of their life course and life cycle without necessarily trying to increase the length of their life span and are not trying to unnaturally or unethically extend the length of the attending relationship/process.
2. Understanding and experiencing that one way that human beings can attain 'immortality' is by fully identifying with/*as* that which is never born and never dying, timeless and eternal, i.e., the Ultimate Reality of Eternal Tao.

Narrative 80
Sacrificing and Benefiting

Yang Chu says that ancient ones say that if people did not sacrifice a single strand of their hair to save the world, then life would be less complicated. He continues by saying that this means that the integrity and wholeness of our human body is important to maintain and sustain; that we often think that we can influence or change the natural course of life by sacrificing something; that we often complicate matters and create problems by thinking that our efforts make a difference or will improve things and that we should leave things alone and let them run their natural course without interfering with them.

Commentary 80 ❖ Sacrificing and Benefiting

Real attenders are:

1. Valuing, honoring, maintaining and sustaining the natural integrity and wholeness of their body as a vehicle for enabling their life to take its natural course and are not necessarily sacrificing its health and well-being for the benefit of human beings or the world.
2. Not having an inflated opinion about being able to influence the lives of human beings and are not devising and implementing agendas to change or to improve them or to interfere with the natural unfolding of their lives.

Narrative 81
Ruling and Tending

Yang Chu is telling a ruler that ruling a country is like tending sheep. Many sheep can be controlled and directed by gently prodding them from behind rather than leading them from ahead.

Yang Chu continues by saying that large animals need to move about in large spaces that match their being, stature, power and strength; that grand music is unfitting for small events and that small knives cannot skin large animals. He adds by saying that successful rulers are not concerned with trivial tasks and do not waste their time on minor achievements.

Commentary 81 ❖ Ruling and Tending

Real attenders are:

1. Guiding human beings from behind and backing them rather than leading them from ahead and possibly blocking or hindering their way of naturally developing, progressing and advancing.
2. Appreciating that the magnitude of the attending relationship/process should correspond with, match and

reflect the magnitude of their personal growth and professional development and are not usually using valuable time and energy dealing with relatively trivial concerns, small matters and minor issues.

Narrative 82
Impermanence of Living

Yang Chu says that what occurs in ancient times is long-forgotten, legendary or imagined; that many events have transpired and many human beings have come and gone; that life is transient and short; and that we should not injure ourselves by trying to achieve some semblance of permanence at the expense of our peacefulness and happiness.

He continues by saying that, as human beings, while we are thought to be the most highly evolved of creatures, we are not privileged over and above animals who, in some ways, appear better equipped to naturally survive and propagate.[12]

Yang Chu adds by saying that we do not own our lives, that we come into existence through the uniting of Yin/Yang Ch'i vital enegies and die when they separate, that we should let life run its course and make the best of it and that if our body is so impermanent, how much moreso are intangibles like name and fame.

Commentary 82 ❖ Impermanence of Living

Real attenders are:

1. Understanding the impermanent nature of human being and living and are appreciating the precious gift of human life temporarily loaned by the natural workings of Heaven-Earth and Yin/Yang Ch'i vital energies.
2. Allowing their life to run its natural cycle and the life of the attending relationship/process to run its natural course and are committed to optimizing the life of both without squandering their vital life/Ch'i energies seeking a famous reputation.

NARRATIVE 83
SEEKING AND SIMPLICITY

Yang Chu says that people typically exhaust themselves seeking and striving for social status, wealth, fame and longevity without realizing that they are sources of cares, worries, anxieties and fears and that only human beings who see through their illusions are free of concerns about negative self-presentations, critical judgments of others, insufficient funds and illness and dying.

He continues by saying that craving and seeking status, wealth, power, reputation and longevity only generate problems and that real happiness and contentment are realized by being true to ourselves and living a simple and carefree life free of competing and of interfering with allowing things to run their natural course.

COMMENTARY 83 ❖ SEEKING AND SIMPLICITY

Real attenders are:

1. Not engaging in the practicing of psychotherapy/counseling seeking, striving and competing to attain social status, amass financial wealth, achieve a famous reputation or extend their professional lives.
2. Not anxious about, or fearful of, the evaluations of other professionals, how much money they earn, how well they are known or how long they have been practicing and are happy, content and free in simply conducting and following the unfolding of the attending relationship/process and allowing and not interfering with just how it is and how it is going.

SECTION EIGHT
THE NATURE OF COMPLETING/SYNCHRONICITY

INTRODUCTION

THE NARRATIVES OF SECTION EIGHT FOCUS ON:

1. NOT VIOLATING THE NATURAL ORDER/TRYING TO IMITATE NATURE/BENEFIT OTHERS/CHANGE THE WORLD.
2. SEEING ESSENCE AND POTENTIALITY BEYOND EXTERNAL APPEARANCES/PARTICULAR CIRCUMSTANCES.
3. NOT PUSHING FOR/GRABBING ONTO/DISPLAYING ABILITY/RANK/WEALTH/POWER/SUCCESS FORMULAS.
4. ATTUNING TO A SINGLE PRINCIPLE/SOURCE/CAUSE AND NOT ONLY ON SYMPTOMS/TECHNIQUES.
5. APPRECIATING THE CIRCUMSTANTIAL RIGHTNESS/TIMELINESS/DESTINY/LUCKINESS OF GOOD FORTUNE.
6. THE ROLE OF UNDERSTANDING/KNOWING IN APPLYING/PERFORMING/SUCCEEDING/MASTERING.
7. NOT BEING PREOCCUPIED WITH THINKING/NAMING/NOT BEING SELF-RIGHTEOUS/SPITEFUL/VENGEFUL.
8. HONESTY/INTEGRITY/INTERCONNECTEDNESS/COMPASSION/CLARITY/TRUST/CALMNESS/CONFIDENCE.
9. REALITIES OF CHANCE CONJUNCTIONS/CONCURRENCES OF EVENTS/COINCIDENCES/SYNCHRONICITIES.
10. ACCEPTING UNEXPECTED HAPPENINGS/SERENDIPITY/NOT GAINING SUCCESS THROUGH PLANNING.
11. ADAPTING TO UNIQUE SITUATIONS/NOT RELYING ON FIXED STANDARDS/UNVARYING PRINCIPLES.
12. SO-CALLED 'REALITIES' OF EXPERIENCE BEING WHAT/HOW WE PERCEIVE/THINK ABOUT THEM.

CH'ENG	CH'UAN
成	全
COMPLETE/COMPLETION FINISH/END FULLY DEVELOPED/WHOLE ACCOMPLISH/ATTAIN PERFECT	COMPLETE/COMPLETION FINISHED/ALL DONE FULL/ENTIRE/TOTAL/ALL/WHOLE ABSOLUTE PERFECT

COMPLETION/CULMINATION

CH'IAO

巧

Coincidental
Accidental/by chance
Opportune/timely
Ingeneous/skillful
Lucky

CHIAO

交

Simultaneous
Intersect/cross
Mutual/reciprocal
Intertwine/interlace
Befriending

CH'IA

恰

Timely
Fitting/appropriate
Union/harmony
Exactly/precisely
Luckily/opportunely

CHI

吉

Lucky
Fortunate
Asupicious
Happy

HSIANG

祥

Lucky/felicitous
Auspicious/propitious
Good omen
Happy

HSING

幸

Lucky/fortunate
Opportune
Favor/prosperity
Happy/joyful

FU

福

Good luck/good fortune
Blessings/prosperity
Happiness/felicity

THE SIMULTANEITY/SYNCHRONICITY AND GOOD FORTUNE/GOOD LUCK OF THE HAPPY/JOYFUL BLESSINGS OF TAO

Narrative 84
Acting and Reacting

Lieh Tzu is studying with his teacher, Wen Tzu, who instructs him that before understanding acting, he needs to know what reacting is and points out how shadows have no control over their movements and only react to their movers.

Wen Tzu further instructs Lieh Tzu that our actions produce reactions in others that follow like shadows, that how we act is how we will be acted upon, that sages are careful in their own actions knowing that others will react to them in predictable ways and that sages are concealing their actions and being unpredictable.

Commentary 84 ❖ Acting and Reacting

Real attenders are:

1. Understanding that their actions inevitably create equivalent and predictable reactions in human beings and are conducting the attending relationship/process carefully, thoughtfully, honestly, kindly, gently, fairly, equally and impartially.
2. Experiencing that, like shadows and echoes cannot produce light and sound because they are effects of them, the personal ego of human beings cannot create a transpersonal Tao-Spirit but, nonetheless, can remember the Tao-Source from whence the ego originated.

Narrative 85
Wealth and Power

Lieh Tzu is asked why people follow the pathway of Tao, citing that it does not make them wealthy or powerful. He replies that human beings follow Tao because they are understanding that pursuing wealth and power lead to downfall and, for that reason, they are not seeking out, grabbing for and clinging onto wealth and power like wild animals.

Commentary 85 ❖ Wealth and Power

Real attenders are:

1. Not expending their vital life energy/Ch'i desiring, coveting, seeking, pursuing, acquiring, possessing, amassing and hoarding financial gain and monetary wealth in their professional practicing of psychotherapy/counseling.
2. Following the pathway of Tao because it is the Ultimate Reality that is originating, nourishing, sustaining, developing, transforming, fulfilling and completing their human lives and the life of the attending relationship/process.

Narrative 86
Understanding and Performing

Lieh Tzu is learning archery and asks his teacher, Wen Tzu, how he can develop and improve his skills. Wen Tzu asks if Lieh Tzu knows how he hits the target and Lieh Tzu answers that he does not know and is directed to practice more.

After some years, Wen Tzu inquires again and this time Lieh Tzu says that he understands how he hits the target and Wen Tzu reminds him that understanding the causal principles of consciously learning and accurately performing archery also apply to regulating oneself and everything else in one's everyday living.

Commentary 86 ❖ Understanding and Performing

Real attenders are:

1. Understanding that the principles and processes of the professional practicing of the real attending relationship/process involve attuning to and according with the dynamic alternating, balancing and reversing of Yin/Yang Ch'i energies and allowing and accompanying the kinetic

flowing, circulating and returning of Wu Wei Ch'i energies.

2. Understanding the intrapsychic principles, interpersonal processes and methodological procedures of conventional psychotherapy/counseling and are also integrating them with complementary transpersonal dimensions of experiencing, enacting and interacting.

Narrative 87
Effective Leadership

Lieh Tzu says that it is useless to discuss Tao with emotionally immature and physically aggressive people because they find it confusing and irrelevant. He continues by saying that wise, effective and successful leaders trust others and choose to delegate responsibilities to the right worthy people who are more mature and stable and have a clear direction in life and an ability to persevere.

Commentary 87 ❖ Effective Leadership

Real attenders are:

1. When directing psychological counseling agencies and clinical treatment centers, usually employing staff members and accepting interns/trainees who are relatively physically stable, emotionally mature, personally goal-directed and professionally diligent workers.
2. When in leadership positions, often effective and successful because of trusting and wisely delegating administrative authority and clinical responsibilities to staff members who are stable, mature, committed, capable and competent.

Narrative 88
Art and Nature

Lieh Tzu tells of an artist who, after spending three years sculpting a piece of jade into a leaf, presents his work of art to a ruler who is unable to distinguish it from real leaves and who is so impressed that he becomes the artist's patron.

Lieh Tzu quips that if Nature took three years to make a leaf, there would be few trees with leaves on them and that Nature/Tao still does a better job of creating works of art.

Commentary 88 ❖ Art and Nature

Real attenders are:

1. Not trying to 'play' Creatrix/Creator/God/Heaven-Earth/Nature/Tao by feeling that the naturally beautiful formings and transformings of human beings engaged in the attending relationship/process are of their own doing.
2. Being natural, creative, innovative and original in their conducting of the attending relationship/process but are not trying to imitate, replicate or compete with the Mysterious originating, Miraculous forming, Marvelous manifesting and Magnificent completing of the experiences of human beings by Heavenly-Earthly Tao and the dynamic-kinetic operations of Yin/Yang Ch'i and Wu Wei Ch'i energies.

Narrative 89
Opinions and Integrity

Lieh Tzu is destitute and hungry and a friend encourages a chief minister to acknowledge his sagehood and attaining Tao by sending him some grain, which he agrees to do. When the minister's courier arrives and presents Lieh Tzu with the gift of grain, he respectfully bows and refuses to accept it. His wife is upset and angry and Lieh Tzu explains that he refuses the gift because dishonor inevitably follows honor and that both are based upon the heresay, opinions, assessments, evaluations and judgments of other people which can endanger him.

Commentary 89 ❖ Opinions and Integrity

Real attenders are:

1. Maintaining the integrity and Virtuosity of their inner Tao-nature and the structure and boundaries of the attending relationship/process by not accepting gifts from the human beings engaged in it.
2. Effectively and successfully conducting the attending relationship/process in ways that do not necessitate human beings acknowledging and reinforcing the beneficial wisdom, in-fluence (in-flowing) and efficacy of their reflections, interpretations, relationships, interactions, responses and interventions.

Narrative 90
Right Place/Right Time

A man with two highly talented sons, one in academic scholarship and the other in military strategy, sends them to two different rulers who are so impressed by the sons that they immediately make one a prince's tutor and the other a commanding general and both quickly rise in status, wealth and power.

After observing the situation, a neighbor, also with two sons of the same talents, consults with the man in order to find out how his own sons might be as fortunate. After their discussing, he sends his two sons to two different rulers who end up violently rejecting them for being totally inappropriate for the needs of their respective countries.

The neighbor accuses the man of tricking him with bad advice and demands an explanation. The man regrets what happened to his neighbor's sons, says that he did not provide a formula or method for success that works in every situation, that the neighbor's sons are as equally talented as his own but that his sons were in the right place at the right time.

Commentary 90 ❖ Right Place/Right Time

Real attenders are:

1. Appreciating that successes in conducting the attending relationship/process may not always be due to their talents, skills, abilities, proficiencies and competencies but rather to the right climate, conducive conditions, appropriate timing and fortuitous circumstances.
2. Not applying fixed formulas and rigid recipes in attempts to create the conditions that guarantee success in conducting the attending relationship/process because they are experiencing that particular understandings and specific methods are not always generalizable and do not always work with every human being in every circumstance.

Narrative 91
Abandoning Coveting

A ruler summons his ministers together, tells them that he is planning to invade a neighboring country and the chief minister breaks out laughing. The shocked ruler demands an explanation and the chief minister relates a story about a man who arranges a secret liason with a woman whom he and his wife had met earlier, sneaks out of their house to engage in the affair and afterward comes back home to discover his wife in bed with another man. The ruler gives up his desire and plans to go after another country's land.

Commentary 91 ❖ Abandoning Coveting

Real attenders are:

1. Content with the number of human beings with whom

they are meeting and serving in their 'caseloads'.
2. Not trying to tap the referral sources of their fellow psychotherapists/counselors in order to acquire more patients/counselees and 'business'.

Narrative 92
Symptoms and Causes

Lieh Tzu tells of the ruler of a crime-ridden country who unsuccessfully tries a number of strategies to control and apprehend criminals. The ruler learns of and summons a man noted for his ability to profile criminal types and sends him to hunt down criminals. The man is very successful and a large number of criminals are captured and imprisoned.

The ruler reports his success in solving his country's crime problem to the sage, Wen Tzu, who comments that criminal activity cannot be stopped by hunting down criminals, that they will keep appearing, that criminality is only a symptom of the country's problem and that the bounty hunter will probably not live for long.

Sure enough, very soon Wen Tzu's prediction comes true and the bounty hunter is murdered by a group of criminals. Wen Tzu counsels the ruler that the best way to reduce criminal activity is to deal with its cause and not its symptoms by employing honest people, educating the public to respect and honor virtue and instilling a sense of integrity in them.

Commentary 92 ❖ Symptoms and Causes

Real attenders are:

1. Working with the deeper underlying causes, and not just treating the presenting symptoms, of the questions, problems, conflicts and issues of human beings engaged in the attending relationship/process.
2. Respecting and honoring, supporting and assisting and

facilitating and guiding the innermost, deepest, centermost, truest and utmost Tao-nature/Virtuosity/Te of human beings in their work of answering questions, solving problems, resolving conflicts and dealing with issues.

Narrative 93
Trusting and Confidence

Confucius and his students come across a woman who is about to dive from the opposite bank of a river into its swiftly rushing currents and caution her not to risk her life doing so. The woman ignores the warnings, dives into the river and leisurely emerges on their side of the river. Amazed at her feat, Confucius asks about her incredible swimming skills and how she is not swept away by, or drowned in, the rapids.

The woman replies that she trusts the water, has confidence in herself, is not afraid because of befriending the water and is able to swim in it without drowning. Confucius asks his students to learn that such trust and confidence also apply to befriending and not fearing human beings.

Commentary 93 ❖ Trusting and Confidence

Real attenders are:

1. Trusting in the structure, boundaries and limits of the attending relationship/process and are confident in themselves even when navigating its rough, swiftly flowing and potentially overwhelming waters.
2. Befriending and not fearing human beings engaged in the attending relationship/process or its potentially risky and challenging realities.

Narrative 94
Keeping a Secret

A ruler, planning to assassinate two of his rivals, consults with Confucius wanting to see if his motives are evident or whether he can keep such a secret. Confucius says that people who listen and understand well and do not talk a lot are probably able to keep and not reveal secrets but that the best way to keep a secret is not to act on it.

Commentary 94 ❖ Keeping a Secret

Real attenders are:

1. Not usually revealing or disclosing their private associations, personal issues and inner work activated by the issues with which human beings engaged in the attending relationship/process are working and the experiences that they are undergoing.
2. Not expressing, acting upon or acting-out the personal material evoked by the nature, focus and actualities of the attending relationship/process and are working inwardly with any of their own issues in their own psychotherapy/counseling.

Narrative 95
Succeeding and Not Displaying

A ruler who is informed that his armies are successful in quickly taking two major cities of a rival state looks worried. When asked about his response, he says that the sudden accomplishment of big events is usually not permanent or long-lasting, that he fears that the victories will not hold and cautions against being excited, becoming negligent and eventually defeated.

Confucius hears of this and says that short-range achievements do not necessarily guarantee long-term success; that the ruler is not proud of, carried away by, reveling in or displaying success; is calm and steady regardless of circumstances and should be able to rule for a long time.

Commentary 95 ❖ Succeeding and Not Displaying

Real attenders are:

1. Not being excited by, proud of, carried away by, reveling in or displaying their successful accomplishments and achievements in conducting the attending relationship/process and are matter-of-factly regarding them as ordinary and everyday occurrences.
2. Understanding that the sudden successful accomplishing of major events and changes occurring in the attending relationship/process may not be permanent or long-lasting and they are accepting them with calmness, equanimity and steadiness.

Narrative 96
Misfortune and Fortune

A family's black cow gives birth to a white calf and they consult Confucius about the omen who tells them that it is a good omen and to thank the Lords of Heaven. The family does so but within a year, the father goes blind. When the black cow births another white calf, the father urges his son to again consult with Confucius which he reluctantly does because of not trusting the sage's previous determination. Confucius again says that the omen is a good one and again to be thankful for the good fortune. However, within another year, the son too goes blind.

As it happens, the family's country is attacked, the father and son have the good fortune of not being conscripted into the army because of their blindness, escape certain death in the vicious bloody battles that follow and, shortly after they are over, recover their sight.

Lieh Tzu says that the wisdom of sages is not always well understood at the time, that it may not be readily apparent if something is good or bad fortune upon first determination and that something that initially appears to be misfortune may later turn out to be good fortune and vice versa. He adds by saying that realizing this assists in not being either depressed or elated about the comings and goings of misfortune and fortune.

COMMENTARY 96 ❖ MISFORTUNE AND FORTUNE

Real attenders are:

1. Not making hasty assessments and premature evaluations about any apparent failures in the conducting of the attending relationship/process which may later prove to be successes.
2. Assisting human beings in keeping an open mind about what is fortune and misfortune in their lives and accepting their life experiences without having fixed beliefs, interpretations, opinions and judgments about whether they are ultimately unfortunate or fortunate ones.

NARRATIVE 97
LUCKY AND UNLUCKY

A wandering acrobat performs juggling swords on tall stilts for a ruler who is so impressed with his abilities that he gives him sizeable rewards. Another wandering acrobat learns of this and offers to demonstrate his abilities on a trapeze to the same ruler. After his performance, the second acrobat is punished for trying to tactically capitalize on the first acrobat's success.

Lieh Tzu says that the first acrobat is lucky and the second acrobat is unlucky; that whether luck is attributed to Heaven-Earth, Nature, God or rulers, it plays a significant determining role in our destiny and that when we understand this, we will be less excited and proud when lucky and less upset and angry when unlucky.

Commentary 97 ❖ Lucky and Unlucky

Real attenders are:

1. Understanding that using the same tactics and strategies in conducting the attending relationship/process can result in both successful and unsuccessful outcomes which may depend upon, and be a matter and result of, the luckiness or unluckiness of circumstances.
2. Understanding that the results and outcomes of the attending relationship/process; whether successful, fortunate and lucky or unsuccessful, unfortunate and unlucky; are a result of the complex interrelationship and interacting of Tao-sourced activity, divine providential blessing or intervention and/or their own doing.

Narrative 98
Beyond Appearances

A horse breeder, renowned for his ability to recognize exceptional horses, is retiring and his ruler, concerned about a successor of equal ability, asks him for a recommendation. The horse breeder says that the finest horses cannot be judged on the basis of appearance, that their potentials must be seen and trained early in order to develop and that he knows of a man with this ability.

The ruler commissions the man who soon finds a prize horse and is asked by the ruler to describe it. The man says that it is a brownish gray mare but when the horse is brought to the stable, it is a dark black stallion. The ruler summons his horse breeder and criticizes him for recommending someone who cannot even tell the correct sex and color of a horse much less train and breed it.

The horse breeder reassures the ruler that his successor possesses abilities that far exceed his own, is completely unconcerned with appearances, does not see female or male, gray or black, and only immediately and directly sees the essential inner Spiritual nature and innate potentials of the horse.

Lieh Tzu says that when the horse is trained by the successor, it becomes the finest horse in the ruler's country.

Commentary 98 ❖ Beyond Appearances

Real attenders are:

1. Generally less overtly focused on and concerned with the external appearances of human beings and are more intuitively aware of their essential inner Spiritual nature and innate human potentials.
2. Competent and proficient in the psychotherapeutic art of effectively and successfully encouraging, supporting, assisting, facilitating and guiding human beings to clearly realize their essential nature and to fully develop their innate potentials.

Narrative 99
Managing and Ruling

A ruler asks a sage about how to govern his country well. The sage replies that she only knows how to manage her life, is responsible for managing Sacred ancestral shrines and knows nothing about government. But she does say that she observes that people who are managing their life well are also ruling a country well and that those who are not managing their life well are not ruling a country well.

Commentary 99 ❖ Managing and Ruling

Real attenders are:

1. Experiencing similarities, parallels and congruences between how well they are managing their personal lives and how well they are conducting their professional lives.
2. Experiencing that the nature, quality, degree, extent and level of their personal development and the talent, skill, ability, proficiency and competency of their professional

work are isomorphically correlated in their art of conducting the attending relationship/ process.

Narrative 100
Trouble and Peace

A sage is telling a wayfarer that rank, ability and wealth are the three things that cause trouble in living by being sources of envy, hatred and resentment. The wayfarer asks if being humble, modest and generous will avoid such trouble and the sage only smiles and remains silent.

Years later, the wayfarer is dying and tells his son that the ruler will likely offer him the same rich, useful and greatly desired central land that he refuses and advises his son to also refuse it in favor of poorer, less useful and less desirable remote land. The son does so and he and his descendents enjoy a long and peaceful life on their land far surpassing the living and dying of central land owners.

Commentary 100 ❖ Trouble and Peace

Real attenders are:

1. Not experiencing any of the difficulties and troubles associated with attaining high-ranking status, displaying exceptional ability and amassing financial wealth in their professional practicing of the attending relationship/ process.
2. Humble, modest and generous human beings who are living peaceful personal lives and enjoying long professional relationships by not engaging in the strivings for, and experiencing the stresses of, fame and wealth.

NARRATIVE 101
NON-ATTACHING AND ATTACHING

A Confucian scholar is traveling through a remote area; bandits rob him of his money, horse and carriage and he resumes his journey on foot as if nothing has happened. The surprised robbers catch up with him and ask why he is not upset over losing his belongings. The scholar replies that virtuous people are not attached to their belongings or to stealing those of other people. The robbers, after thinking that such a wise person will later see to it that they are apprehended, murder him.

Learning of this, a family elder counsels the scholar's brother not to act like such a virtuous scholar if he ever encounters robbers. Shortly afterward, the brother is traveling and is confronted by robbers. Recalling the advice of his elder, he resists the robbers, tries to hold onto his possessions and chases after them when they are taken. The robbers, after considering the man ungrateful for having his life spared and fearing that he will have them tracked down, murder him.

COMMENTARY 101 ❖ NON-ATTACHING AND ATTACHING

Real attenders are:

1. Not attached to holding onto theoretical knowledge, technical skills and the human beings engaged in the attending relationship/process and do not have to consider, or try to create conditions or to devise strategies, to prevent losing them.
2. Experiencing that there is no strategy, or its opposite, for maintaining the structure and function of the attending relationship/process, e.g., being non-attached or attached, that effectively guarantees that human beings will not lose insights, changes, improvements and progress.

Narrative 102
Accidental Retribution

A very wealthy man regularly throws large and lavish parties for reveling guests. One evening, their shouting frightens a hawk hovering near the balcony that drops a dead rat it is carrying which accidently falls onto the leader of a group of soldiers standing in the street below.

The leader says that he has long been exasperated with the proud, pretentious and arrogant behavior of the rich man who now throws a dead rat onto him. To avenge the perceived humiliating insult, later that evening, the leader and soldiers sneak into the man's mansion and murder him and his whole family.

Commentary 102 ❖ Accidental Retribution

Real attenders are:

1. At appropriate times, clarifying, acknowledging and resolving any negative and upsetting countertransference feelings toward human beings engaged in the attending relationship/ process by honestly disclosing and constructively working with them rather than witholding and harboring them.
2. Not expressing or acting-out any intensely negative or upsetting projective identifications or countertransference feelings toward human beings in the attending relationship/process and are working with them in their own psychotherapy/counseling.

Narrative 103
Identity and Reality

A man faints while traveling on a remote road and is noticed by a robber who tries to revive him by offering him water and some food. When the man awakens fully, he recognizes the robber and refuses to be helped by him, saying that he is a virtuous man who accepts nothing from criminals. The man tries to throw up the food he is given and chokes to death.

Lieh Tzu says that, even though the helping man is identified as a criminal, his actions are not criminal and that, because of his self-righteousness, the helped man confuses the identity of the helping man and the reality of his assistance and that is his ultimate undoing.

Commentary 103 ❖ Identity and Reality

Real attenders are:

1. Human beings of generally real and humble Virtuosity rather than self-righteously judgmental 'virtue'.
2. Able, if and when necessary, to accept, and to not refuse, assistance from human beings without judging their personal character or social identity.

Narrative 104
Unnatural Vengence

An unappreciated servant resigns from a ruler's staff and prefers to live as a hermit foraging for food rather than eating that of the ruler. Shortly thereafter, the ruler is attacked by rivals and the former servant rushes in to help defend him. His friends are puzzled by his risking his life for a ruler who does not value him. The former servant explains that he leaves the ruler because he is shamed by him and sees an opportunity to shame the ruler, and to set an example for other unappreciative rulers, by risking dying for him.

Lieh Tzu says that risking our life for someone who values us and not risking dying for someone who does not value us is according with the natural way of Tao and doing the opposite for vengence goes against the natural order of Tao.

Commentary 104 ❖ Unnatural Vengence

Real attenders are:

1. Valuing and appreciating human beings and are not accidently rewounding them by inadvertently faulting or unwittingly shaming them for any human limitations or failures that they are experiencing and undergoing.
2. Transcending either valuing or devaluing human beings, or being valued or devalued by them, and are not violating professional ethics by harboring, expressing or acting-out any vindictive, vengeful or retaliatory countertransference feelings and projective identifications.

Narrative 105
A Single Principle

Yang Chu's neighbor loses a sheep; friends, relatives and Yang Chu's staff all go off to search for it and Yang Chu questions why so many people are going. The neighbor says that many people are needed because there are many forks in the road that need to be explored.

The search party returns without having found the sheep and Yang Chu says that this is due to their confusion about too many paths to take, being overwhelmed by too many alternatives and choices to make and having to turn back. He continues by saying that finding Tao involves having only one principle and focusing on only one method, following them to completion and discovering their Source.

Commentary 105 ❖ A Single Principle

Real attenders are:

1. Not attempting to assist human beings in finding answers to questions, solutions to problems, resolutions of conflicts and completions of issues through the use of too many alternatives and choices that overwhelm them and fail to work.

2. Usually reaching and discovering the deeper foundation, core and source of understanding and experiencing the issues of human beings by focusing on and following a single principle and a single method to their completion, i.e., the way and path of Tao and the operating of dynamically alternating Yin/Yang Ch'i and kinetically flowing Wu Wei Ch'i energies.

Narrative 106
Misunderstood Behavior

Yang Chu's brother leaves the house wearing a white suit and, knowing that in the meantime the courtyard is muddied because of heavy rain, returns wearing a black suit. His dog barks and growls at him and he is about to harshly discipline the dog but Yang Chu points out that the dog is naturally surprised and confused as he, the brother, would be if the dog had gone out white and come back black.

Commentary 106 ❖ Misunderstood Behavior

Real attenders are:

1. Not being confused, or necessarily surprised, by the seeming radical changes and transformings that human beings are making and exhibiting and are, instead, exploring and understanding their causes.
2. Transcending the dualistic black-white, mutually exclusive and either-or Yin/Yang differences of the experiences, changes and transformings of human beings by understanding and experiencing them in relation to the larger encompassing and unifying context of nondual Tao.

Narrative 107
Knowing and Applying

A ruler summons a man who knows the secrets of immortality but the man dies before being reached by the messenger. Another man wants to learn the secrets of immortality from a hermit and laments the hermit's untimely death and losing the opportunity.

A philosopher considers the so-called immortals to be frauds since they both die but Lieh Tzu's teacher disagrees. He says that some people know principles but cannot apply them and other people can apply principles without knowing what they are and that it is not unusual for mortals to possess knowledge about immortality.

Lieh Tzu says that it is rare that someone both knows the theory and is able to apply it and that it is difficult to tell if it is easier to derive action from knowledge or to induce knowledge from action.

Commentary 107 ❖ Knowing and Applying

Real attenders are:

1. Well versed in psychological theories and are able to apply them to, integrate them with and implement them in the psychotherapeutic conducting and practicing of the attending relationship/process.
2. Experiencing that some of their professional colleagues are theoretically sophisticated but unable to apply their knowledge in practice and that others are technically accomplished without necessarily being theoretically knowledgeable.

Narrative 108
Real Compassion

A ruler encourages his subjects to present him with live doves to annually celebrate New Year's Day and rewards them according to the number of doves that they bring in. A guest inquires about the ritual and the ruler says that New Year's Day is a good time to compassionately honor and value the lives of all living beings by releasing the doves.

The guest then points out that, because people are rewarded for the number of doves that they bring in, they compete to capture as many doves as possible and that many doves are injured or die in the process. The guest adds by saying that the ruler can show real compassion for life by issuing an order banning the hunting and capturing of doves.

Commentary 108 ❖ Real Compassion

Real attenders are:

1. Not valuing or identifying with human beings who are celebrating the life of one living being through paradoxically causing the death of another living being.
2. Really and truly compassionate human beings who value, honor and respect the lives of human beings and all living beings daily and directly without instituting or performing ritual observances only on one certain day.

Narrative 109
Who Is Eating Whom?

A ruler is holding a huge banquet attended by many guests. When fish and fowl are served, he raises his head, looks skyward and thanks Heaven for beneficently creating and providing the food for everyone to eat. The guests all nod in agreement except for the young son of one of the guests who voices his disagreement.

He points out that all beings are the creation of Heaven-Earth, that one is not more valuable than another and that none are created for the benefit of any other much less in order to be eaten by them. The boy adds by saying that if we, as human beings, say that fish and fowl are created for us to eat; we have to say that we, as human beings, are created for mosquitoes and gnats to bite our skin and tigers and wolves to eat our flesh.

Commentary 109 ❖ Who Is Eating Whom?

Real attenders are:

1. Not prioritizing human being over the existing of other living beings or feeling that they are created for our benefit and are not considering human beings engaged in the attending relationship/process as being present for their benefit.
2. Understanding and not interfering with the essential interdependent and reciprocal complementarity and the ecological balancing and harmonizing interrelationships of human beings and other living beings in the planetary ecosystem.

Narrative 110
The Way We Think About It

A poor man keeps begging for a living in the same local market but people tire of helping him. He takes a menial stable job and is ridiculed by the market-goers but says that his job is more honest than shamefully begging.

Another man collects what people drop in the street; adds torn money notes, unclaimed pawnshop receipts and old lottery tickets to his collection and tells his neighbors that soon he will be wealthy.

Another man has a sycamore tree, is told by a neighbor that it is unlucky, chops it down and stores the logs behind his house. The neighbor steals the logs and the man feels tricked into cutting down the tree for the neighbor's firewood.

Another man loses his axe and suspects that the neighbor boy stole it. He observes the boy's looks, demeanor and behavior and is convinced that he stole the axe. Soon after, he finds the axe in his garden and when he sees the boy again, nothing suggests that he would steal an axe.

Lieh Tzu says that whether or not an activity is shameful, whether or not we are poor or wealthy, whether or not people are crafty and whether or not someone looks suspicious or guilty all depend upon the way we perceive, think about and interpret it in our minds with clarity or with distortions.

Commentary 110 ❖ The Way We Think About It

Real attenders are:

1. Committed to honesty and integrity in conducting their professional practices of the attending relationship/process and are not perpetuating an illusion of becoming wealthy through it.
2. Not tricked or fooled into necessarily believing what some human beings are presenting to them but also are not necessarily doubting their intentions, suspecting their motives or making unquestioned projections onto, or judgments about, them based upon their appearance, body language and/or behavior.

Narrative 111
Cloudy and Clear

A man is so completely preoccupied with thinking about avenging his father's murderer that he is unaware of holding his walking stick upside down. It pierces his cheek when he leans on it and he does not even notice the bleeding.

Another man is so totally obsessed with thinking about having money and being wealthy that he goes to the market and grabs a bag of gold from the stall of a gold dealer in broad daylight with everyone around, runs off and is quickly caught.

Lieh Tzu says that the two men are so engrossed in their own thoughts and that their minds are so set on things that they ignore their surroundings and everything else is obscured. He continues by saying that people often trip over things, bump into posts and step into holes because they are so preoccupied with their own thoughts, out of touch with themselves and not seeing the whole picture of what is right in front of them.

Lieh Tzu adds by saying that it is dangerous when we are too involved in a situation, when we cannot see straight and clearly and when obvious things are cloudy or not noticed.[13]

Commentary 111 ❖ Cloudy and Clear

Real attenders are:

1. Often one-pointed and single-minded in focusing on human beings and their issues but are not so preoccupied that they cannot at the same time clearly see most all of the other constituents, characteristics, attributes and qualities of the surrounding circumstances of the attending relationship/process as it unfolds, proceeds, changes, develops and progresses.
2. Not so preoccupied with their own thoughts and feelings, associations and reflections, plans and strategies, methods and techniques and goals and objectives that they are unavailable and inaccessible to human beings or unable to accept, attune to, allow, accord with, accompany and abide in the natural unfolding and transforming of the attending relationship/process.

SHENG

圣

Sacred/wise
Sage/saint
Holy/saintly
Spiritual/divine

CHEN

真

True/authentic
Real/genuine
Natural state
Spiritual/divine

SHIH

實

Real/actual
True/genuine
Authentic/sincere
Solid/substantial

JEN

人

Human being
Person/people
Humankind
Populace/masses

**THE SACRED/WISE/TRUE/REAL/
SPIRITUAL NATURE/EMBODIMENT/
PERSONIFICATION OF HUMAN BEING**

CONCLUSION

Applications

The following are some applications of the eight principal experiential concepts to conducting the practicing of the attending relationship/process of psychotherapy/counseling.

Tao/Ultimate Reality

1. No-Thing being/being no-'thing-other'/Tao-sourced interbeing.
2. Not only past history/etiology of presenting symptoms/issues.
3. Non-relationally separated 'being' as the open ground of unity/oneness.
4. Not professional persona/rigid roles/transference relationships.
5. Appropriate availability/accessibilty/self-disclosure/communing.
6. Context/frame/psychotherapeutic principle/path/synchronicity.
7. Being-with human beings engaged in the attending relationship/process.

Te/Unique Virtuosity

1. No-Thing knowing/knowing no-'thing-content'/Tao-sourced knowing.
2. Not only diagnostic assessment/interpretation/rational insight.
3. Non-mentally construed 'knowing' as the open ground of clarity/clearness.
4. Not preferred theories/abstract concepts/intellectualized explanations.
5. Relevant/eclectic/holistic/concrete understandings/constituting.

6. Talent/artistry/psychotherapeutic presence/potency/sagacity.
7. Letting-be of human beings engaged in the attending relationship/process.

Yin/Yang Ch'i/Dynamic Bipolarity

1. No-Thing having/having no 'thing-goods'/Tao-sourced having.
2. Not only case formulation/clinical judgments/emotional catharsis.
3. Non-emotionally desired 'having' as the open ground of vacuity/emptiness.
4. Not monologues/unilateral interactions/preferred treatment agendas.
5. Bipolar nature of issues/problems/conflicts/experiences/corresponding.
6. Change/transformation/psychotherapeutic polarity/parity/simplicity.
7. Letting-go of human beings engaged in the attending relationship/process.

Wu Wei Ch'i/Kinetic Fluidity

1. No-Thing doing/doing no 'thing-deeds'/Tao-sourced doing.
2. Not only treatment plans/intervention strategies/prognostic outcomes.
3. Non-volitionally enacted 'doing' as the open ground of tranquility/stillness.
4. Not preferred programs/fixed techniques/treatment interventions.
5. Improvised methods/process-generated goals/objectives/collaborating.
6. Yielding/flowing/psychotherapeutic process/proceeding/synergy.
7. Going-with human beings engaged in the attending relationship/process.

Ch'i/Vital Energy

1. Conserving/not wasting vital energy working with irrelevant concerns/issues/material.
2. Conscious awareness of energy level/dissipation/draining/depletion/burnout.
3. Allowing vital energies to naturally unblock/balance rather than manipulating them.
4. Energy/vitality/vibrancy/psychotherapeutic patterns/pathways/sustaining.

Wan Wu/Phenomenal Diversity

1. Staying within the phenomenological frame of reference of human beings.
2. Making/noting/utilizing behavioral observations of nonverbal body language.
3. Valuing whatever phenomena are manifesting in the attending relationship/process.
4. Content/material/psychotherapeutic plurality/panorama/sacralizing.

Tzu Jan/Natural Spontaneity

1. Suspending past clinical experience/treatment presuppositions/preconceptions.[14]
2. Appreciating unplanned/spontaneous/synchronistic/serendipitous happenings.
3. Being awake/aware of/alert/attentive to constant/continual/continuous presencing.
4. Not interfering with the natural/free unfolding of the attending relationship/process.
5. Improvisation/innovation/psychotherapeutic presencing/'playing'/serendipity.

Tao Jen/Consummate Humanity

1. Not engaging in professional practice to meet personal needs/accrue financial wealth.
2. Impartially/empathically engaging in intersubjective

relating/dialogical communicating.

3. Deeply/fully appreciating the precious blessing/ gift/ opportunity of human being/living.
4. Being personally/professionally committed to serving/ assisting/benefiting human beings.
5. Open/wholeheartedness/compassion/psychotherapeutic partnering/participating/sanctity.

Psychotherapy/Counseling

Psychotherapy/counseling is an available resource and accessible opportunity for serving, supporting, assisting, facilitating and guiding individual human beings in answering the questions, solving the problems, resolving the conflicts, healing the separations and dealing with the issues that are preventing them from living a more vital, functional, optimal, fulfilling, intimate, peaceful, liberated and/or happy life.

While initially a professional outgrowth of the medical and psychiatric professions and their ideologies; traditional and conventional psychotherapy/counseling practice has become more associated with and dependent upon the theoretical formulations, evidence-based research, scientific findings and methodological techniques of the behavioral and human sciences and the liberal and expressive arts.

More recently; the alternative, complementary and integral approaches of existential, phenomenological, humanistic and transpersonal psychotherapy/counseling include the wisdom teachings and meditative practices of Eastern Spiritual and philosophical traditions such as Hinduism, Buddhism, Sufism and Taoism. The current focus, scope, utility and benefit of individual psychotherapy/counseling practice range from concerns with our psychophysical integrity and health, through our psychosocial relationships and psychological development to our psychospiritual reality and evolution.

However, traditional/conventional and even alternative/

complementary/holistic/integrative psychotherapy/counseling mostly focus upon levels of observation and kinds of issues and work through forms of conduct and methods of treatment that are within the arena and scope of the physical health, mental stability, emotional regulation, social integration, self development and general well-being of the ego-states and ego-identifications of human beings and typically do not involve the direct application and explicit use of the wisdom teachings and meditative practices of Eastern Spiritual traditions for Self-awakening and Self-transforming.

As such, they serve the necessary and vital function of healing the ego-woundings, ego-deficiencies and ego-weaknesses and developing the ego-structures, ego-functions and ego-strengths that are essential preconditions for, and existential precursors of, opening the way to allowing human beings to begin to engage in the deeper and more disciplined and rigorous training, cultivating and practicing involved in the explicit work of Spiritual awakening and evolving and the enSouling process that essentially and necessarily involve the tutelage, mentoring and guidance of Spiritual masters and teachers rather than psychotherapists and counselors.

In the psychotherapeutic commentaries of this rendition, psychotherapy/counseling has been characterized as 'the attending relationship/process', since its conduct, efficiency, effectiveness and benefit are essentially contingent upon psychotherapists/counselors being able to openly, closely, deeply and fully attend to, connect with, participate with and commune with human beings engaged in its ongoing proceeding and natural unfolding.

Appendixes One and Two of this rendition contain succinct references to, summaries of and applications of; the nature, characteristics, attributes, qualities and activities of a way of being and living and a way of conducting and practicing the attending relationship/process portrayed in each of the narratives and described in each of the commentaries.

Patients/Counselees

So-called patients/counselees are, first and foremost, human beings with given personal names and are not only role-designated patients, counselees, clients or 'cases'. In the commentaries of this rendition, they have been referred to as 'human beings' or 'human beings engaged in the attending relationship/process'.

Although they may not have been regarded and treated as such or believe and experience themselves to be as such; human beings engaging in the attending relationship/process are legitimate, valid, significant, worthwhile, valuable, intelligent, capable, functional and whole human beings in their own right who are deserving of being openly welcomed, received and accepted; closely attended, listened and related to and fully encouraged, supported and assisted with dignity, respect, safety, trust, interest, compassion and kindness.

Unless referred or mandated, human beings voluntarily enter into psychotherapy/counseling usually because they cannot find or make use of resources within themselves or among other human beings in their lives that enable them to cope and deal with not authentically being themselves and/or not optimally living a meaningful, satisfying, intimate and/or productive life. Human beings are engaging in psychotherapy/counseling for a wide variety of reasons and conditions, e.g., to:

Answer questions	**Understand self**	**Heal woundings**
Solve problems	**Meet challenges**	**Improve health**
Resolve conflicts	**Complete objectives**	**Develop self**
Manage issues	**Realize potentials**	**Live life**
Overcome obstacles	**Actualize opportunities**	**Enhance growth**
Change patterns	**Achieve success**	**Raise consciousness**
Control behaviors	**Manifest hopes**	**Be free/happy/etc.**

And to mitigate/alleviate/ameliorate/relieve/reduce/end the pain/anguish/misery/suffering of:

Bipolar cyclings	**Panic attacks/fears**	**Delusions/hallucinations**
Flashbacks/nightmares	**Phobias/worries**	**Suicidal ideation/impulses**
Anxiety/tension	**Addictive behavior**	**Obsessions/compulsions**
Depression/grief	**Anger/frustration**	**Doubts/insecurities**
Personality disorders	**Shame/guilt**	**Inadequacies/inferiorities**

Enervating/exhausting/debilitating/disabling/chronic/ terminal physical illnesses et al.[15]

Human beings engaging in the attending relationship/process of psychotherapy/counseling are capable of co-creating, establishing and sustaining collaborative and cooperative therapeutic relationships and alliances with real attenders that are experienced as being relevant, meaningful, effective, successful, beneficial and useful. They are responsible for the manner in which and the depth and extent to which they are regarding, understanding, relating to, caring for, experiencing, being, living, sharing and enjoying the unique reality and actuality of their individual human nature and Self and the precious gift and treasure of their individual human life and Soul.

Furthermore, the psychological health, integration and well-being of human beings clearly, deeply, fully and freely engaged in the attending relationship/process constitute the solid foundational ground, stable regulatory center and consciously open spaciousness that are preconditions for engaging in any continuing work on Spiritual awakening, Soulful living and Human evolving.

Psychotherapists/Counselors

So-called psychotherapists/counselors also are, first and foremost, human beings with given names and are not only role-designated psychotherapists, counselors, therapists and 'doctors'. In the commentaries of this rendition, they have been referred to as 'real attenders' in keeping with the identifying of sages in *The Lieh Tzu* text as real/actual human beings/Shih Jen.

Real attenders are human beings who typically are responding to a calling to serve human beings in a professional vocation similar to that of psychotherapy/counseling, often from an early age. They are characteristically committed to and engaged in conducting the attending relationship/process in a morally ethical, personally responsible and professionally accountable manner and without ego-centric needs for, investments in or attachments to name, status, reputation, fame, gain, wealth or power.

Real attenders are appreciating the precious gift of human incarnation and life; are acknowledging its brevity and transiency; are accepting the uniquely embodied, individualized and personified Tao-nature of human beings and are attuning to, according with, allowing and accompanying the attending relationship/process as it naturally unfolds, proceeds, develops and completes itself with a minimal amount of controlling, directing, intervening, interfering, manipulating and/or forcing.

Real attenders are conducting the attending relationship/process through the following four modes of being:

1. LETTING-BE — abstaining from trying to change/alter/modify/convert human beings.
2. LETTING-GO — relinquishing attaching to/retaining/overidentifying with human beings.
3. GOING-WITH — sourcing the actions/activities of human beings in the operating of Tao/Ch'i.
4. BEING-WITH — collaborating with human beings intersubjectively in therapeutic alliances.[16]

Real attenders embrace eclectic-holistic theories and utilize complementary-integrative methodologies. They are not invested in, or attached to, particular preferred treatment models, agendas, formulas, strategies, techniques, regimens or outcomes and impartially relate to, and work within, the unique phenomenological frame of reference, subjective context of experiencing and natural constitution and temperments of human beings. They often do so through spontaneously creative and innovative reflections, interpretations, relationships, interactions, responses and interventions which are, nonetheless, necessary, essential, appropriate, fitting and/or suitable.

Real attenders embody an openness that is characterized by:

1. A mental clearness of non-knowing 'contents' and 'clutter'.
2. An emotional emptiness of non-having 'goods' and 'baggage'.
3. A volitional stillness of non-doing 'deeds' and 'feats'.
4. A relational oneness of non-being 'others' and 'strangers'.

and that enables them to receive, reflect, respond to and reside with human beings just *as* who they are being, just *as* what and how they are doing and just *as* when and where they are going.

Real attenders are fundamentally and quintessentially humble, genuine, authentic and sincere human beings who are dedicated to serving, encouraging, supporting, assisting, facilitating and guiding the wayfaring journeying of human beings throughout the life course and life cycle of the attending relationship/process. They are guiding from below, behind and between rather than leading from above, ahead and beyond in ways that human beings experience as being of real, actual and practical meaning, use and benefit in living their ordinary and everyday lives.

The sheer and utter power of the presence alone of real attenders is naturally exerting a harmonizing and transforming in-fluence (in-flowing) upon and within human beings.

To a more advanced degree and evolved extent, real attenders are identifying *as* Tao and its dynamic Yin/Yang Ch'i and kinetic Wu Wei Ch'i vital energies as they naturally fluctuate, transform, alternate, balance, center, reverse, flow, circulate, cycle and return. Through active listening, empathic attuning, synergic interacting and rhythmic entraining; they are yielding to, joining with and following the natural being and experiencing of human beings and the natural unfolding and proceeding of the attending relationship/process; precisely, accurately and consistently with focused concentration, intuitive awareness and illuminated insight; with calmness, equanimity and stability and without stress, conflict or struggle.

In terms of the essential wisdom contained in *The Lieh Tzu* text, real attenders are following the natural law, natural order, natural way, natural unfolding, natural process, natural course and natural cycle of the blessed gift and precious treasure of human being and living. And they are accepting, understanding and appreciating that the fortunate occurrences and successful outcomes of the healing, transforming, developing and evolving of human beings are often due to the good luck and opportune timing of fortunate converging and coincidental factors, circumstances and happenings that are fundamentally, essentially and ultimately beyond the control of will power and conscious effort.

In conducting the attending relationship/process, real attenders are characterized by the following 'less' and 'more' qualities and activities that are organized in terms of the four principal experiential concepts and modalities of Te, Yin/Yang Ch'i, Wu Wei Ch'i and Tao.

Te/Noetics	**Te/Noetics**
Less	***More***
Knowing 'about'/reckoning/construing.	Letting-be/receiving/comprehending.
Abstracting/analyzing.	Concretizing/synthesizing.
Defining/diagnosing.	Describing/normalizing.
Interpreting/explaining.	Witnessing/reflecting.
Concluding/speculating.	Exploring/discovering.
Verbalizing.	Listening.

Yin/Yang Ch'i/Dynamics	**Yin/Yang Ch'i Dynamics**
Less	***More***
Having 'of'/retaining/claiming.	Letting-go/complementing/reciprocating.
Unilaterality/partiality.	Bipolarity/impartiality.
Assessing/evaluating.	Aligning/attuning.
Judging/weighting.	Balancing/centering.
Formulating/associating.	Equalizing/according.
Monologuing.	Dialoguing.

Wu Wei Ch'i Kinetics	**Wu Wei Ch'i Kinetics**
Less	***More***
Doing 'of'/regulating/contriving.	Going-with/responding/complying.
Planning/strategizing.	Developing/proceeding.
Controlling/directing.	Yielding/allowing.
Initiating/challenging.	Supporting/replying.
Implementing/executing.	Following/guiding.
Intervening.	Unfolding.

Tao/Ontics	**Tao/Ontics**
Less	***More***
Being 'apart'/reducing/confronting	Being-with/residing/communing.
Externalizing/objectifying.	Internalizing/intersubjectivity.
Distancing/separating.	Sharing/participating.
Dividing/fragmenting.	Connecting/joining.
Formalizing/ritualizing.	Uniting/integrating.
Isolating.	Disclosing.

Notes

1. The Chinese characters interspersed throughout this rendition are defined by their etymological radicals and phonetics and their extended philosophical meanings.

2. Lieh Tzu, who lives during the 4th Century BCE (c. 350 BCE), reportedly is born in the feudal state of Cheng, however, the historical dates of that state are variously given in references as c. 774-500/806-375 BCE. Perhaps reference is being made to a geographical area of China that previously had been the feudal state of Cheng.

3. Lao Tzu (c. 6th Century BCE) is a philosopher contemporary of Confucius/K'ung Fu Tzu (c. 551-479 BCE) living during the Spring/Ch'un and Autumn/Ch'iu period (c. 770-476 BCE) of the Eastern Chou Dynasty (c. 770-221 BCE) and is the purported author of the *Tao Te Ching*. See the companion book *Lao Tzu's Tao Te Ching. Psychotherapeutic Commentaries. A Wayfaring Counselor's Rendering of the Tao Virtuosity Experience.* He appears in several of the narratives of *The Lieh Tzu* text.

4. Wen Shih Tzu (c. 5th Century BCE) is a disciple of Lao Tzu, and a teacher of Lieh Tzu, and is the purported author of *The Further Teachings of Lao Tzu: Understanding the Mysteries.* He appears in several of the narratives of *The Lieh Tzu* text.

5. Chuang Tzu (c. 365-286 BCE) is a philosopher contemporary of Lieh Tzu living during the Warring States period (c. 475-221 BCE) of the Eastern Chou Dynasty (c. 770-221 BCE) and is the purported author of the first seven Inner Chapters/Nei P'ien of *The Chuang Tzu* text. See the companion book *Chuang Tzu's Nei P'ien. Psychotherapeutic Commentaries. A Wayfaring*

Counselor's Rendering of the Seven Interior Records. He is mentioned in one narrative in Section One of *The Lieh Tzu* text.

6. Confucius/K'ung Fu Tzu (c. 551-479 BCE) is a philosopher contemporary of Lao Tzu (c. 6th Century BCE). He appears in various narratives throughout *The Lieh Tzu* text and 'Confucius' is the title of Section Four of the text. The Confucian 'way' is one of creating and maintaining cultural reform and social order through formalizing, teaching and learning the moral virtues of benevolence/Jen, righteousness/I and propriety/Li and is often contrasted with the Taoist Way that is one of living and sharing cultural realities and social changes through embodying, being and enjoying the natural Virtuosity of their goodness, softness and kindness.

7. Yang Chu (c. 350 BCE) is a philosopher contemporary of Lieh Tzu and Chuang Tzu. He appears in various narratives throughout *The Lieh Tzu* text and 'Yang Chu' is the title of Section Seven of the text. The 'way' of Yang Chu is one of enjoying and making the most out of our precious, transient and short lives and not sacrificing physical integrity, suppressing natural instincts and/or denying sensual pleasures. This section is regarded as 'hedonistic' by Graham and, also, is not included in a selection of the Giles translation of *The Lieh Tzu* text.

8. During the microlab basic counseling skills training of psychology graduate students, fully attending and clearly listening are found to create experiences of safe contact and deep connection that open the way to rapport, self-disclosure, genuine communication, self-awareness, insight and expression without the necessity of utilizing other facilitative skills.

9. Chuang Tzu is only referred to in Wong's hermeneutic explication of *The Lieh Tzu* text and not in the Giles or Graham translations.

10. Real attenders are identifying *as* Original/Constant Tao and its dynamic Yin/Yang Ch'i and kinetic Wu Wei Ch'i energies which are constituting the efficacious agency and potency of their inner Tao-nature/Virtuosity and the principal catalytic influence and harmonizing and transformative power of their presence alone in conducting the attending relationship/process.

11. The dates given for when Lao Tzu (c. 6th Century BCE) and Yang Chu (c. 4th Century BCE) live do not coincide; unless either their reported lifetimes are historically misdated, Lao Tzu is an immortal, 'Lao Tzu' is a generic name for any 'old philosopher' or the author of the narrative is imaginatively inventing and characterizing their relationship as the symbolically personified meeting of conscious social 'wisdom' and unconscious individual 'freedom'.

12. I believe that we can consider, as 'intelligent', the incredible instinct-based survival and proliferative value of the adaptive mutability and viability of micro-organisms, the antibiotic-resistant strains of bacteria and viruses and the specialized colonial social organization of hymenopterous insects, e.g., ants and bees.

13. Absorbing distractions are particularly risky and dangerous for individuals who are text messaging or using smart phones while walking, running, jogging, bicycling and/or driving motor vehicles.

14. This attitude and approach are fundamentally ones of the philosophical discipline and methodology of empirical/existential and ontological/transcendental phenomenology, whereby any presuppositions and preconceptions of phenomena are suspended and 'bracketed out' in order to be open to receive the 'givenness' of their explicit existential presentation to conscious awareness and their implicit intentional constitution by the Transcendental Ego just as they are.

15. A longer listing of typical presenting issues, concerns and ongoing focuses of psychotherapy/counseling is found on page 211 of the companion book *Lao Tzu's Tao Te Ching. Psychotherapeutic Commentaries. A Wayfaring Counselor's Rendering of the Tao Virtuosity Experience.*

16. Some clarification needs to be provided with respect to understanding 'letting-be/accepting', 'letting-go/according' and 'going-with/allowing'. These states, characteristics, qualities and activities of being are not ones of a laissez-faire, 'anything and everything is okay and permitted' and 'doing nothing' with respect to behavior, relationships and actions. The attending relationship/process is clearly and consistently structured in terms of boundaries, limits and permissable behavior that insure the safety and protect the integrity of human beings engaged in it and of wise/true/real attenders conducting it. Such boundary-keeping and limit-setting guarantee that actions will be essential, necessary, appropriate, fitting and suitable

The key factor with respect to non-interfering, non-interrupting and non-intervening is in clearly considering and fully understanding the point, place and time of 'accepting', 'according' and 'allowing', e.g., psychotherapists/counselors are necessarily and appropriately accepting, according with and allowing their non-accepting of, non-according with, non-allowing of and stopping of any aggressively violent or blatantly sexual actions toward them or of any overtly harmful or self-destructive behavior of human beings toward themselves.

'Accepting of', 'according with' and 'allowing of' more aptly apply to the nature of the appearances, personalities and life styles of human beings; to the content of their feelings, thoughts and verbalizations and to the forms of their behaviors, relationships and actions that are professionally, necessarily, appropriately, responsibly and accountably limited, controlled and regulated by reality, reason, rationality, ethics and morality.

17. In some ways; classifying, categorizing, labeling and defining may appear to be inconsistent with, and antithetical to, the Spirit of Taoism. However, language and its wording do correspond with and evoke the realities and actualities of human being, living and experiencing toward which they point and are not only and simply mental abstractions, conceptual objectifications and nominal designations. The material presented throughout this rendition and contained in these two epilogues is offered in the Spirit of Lieh Tzu's name, i.e., of the Chinese character 'Lieh', meaning 'to variously set out/list/arrange in order/classify'.

18. There is a correlation between the four meditative practices of Heart-Mind Fasting, Sitting Forgetting, Origin Wandering and Tao Residing and their respective Non-Being/Wu states and Being/Yu states referred to in the companion book *Chuang Tzu's Nei P'ien. Psychotherapeutic Commentaries. A Wayfaring Counselor's Rendering of the Seven Interior Records* as follows:

MEDITATIVE PRACTICE	*Heart-Mind Fasting/Hsin Chai* Letting-Be/Abstaining	*Sitting Forgetting/Tso Wang* Letting-Go/Relinquishing
WU STATE	Non-Knowing/Wu Chih/Shih	Non-Having/Wu Yu
YU STATE	Clearness/Ch'ing	Emptiness/Hsu
MEDITATIVE PRACTICE	*Origin Wandering/Yuan Yu* Going-With/Following	*TaoResiding/Tao/Ch'u/Chu Ch'u* Being-With/Joining
WU STATE	Non-Doing/Wu Wei	Non-Being/Wu Yu
YU STATE	Stillness/An/Ning/P'ing	Oneness/I

19. The following specifies the nature, characteristics, attributes and qualities of the Mystery of originating, the Miracles of forming, the Marvels of manifesting and the Magnificence of completing of human being and living.

Mystery of Originating/Conception
A being/something from No-thing
HSUAN — mysterious/secret
玄
dark/black
deep/profound
subtle/abstruse

Miracles of Forming/Gestation
Creating of an 'edge' to a being
CHIAO — border/boundary
徼
edge/limit
frontier/margin
outer form

Marvels of Manifesting/Parturition
Presencing of the actualities of a being
MIAO — marvelous/wonderful
妙
beautiful/graceful
excellent/admirable
subtle/splendid

Magnificence of Completing/Maturation
Culminating of the living of a being
HUA — magnificent/elegant
華
splendid/glorious
beautiful/flowering
consummating/culminating

20. Considering Tao and Te/Virtuosity, respectively, as our Human Spirit and Human Soul and regarding wayfaring as the journeying of our Human Soul throughout the human life course, life cycle and life span are the principal focuses of Soul-work, Soul-making and the enSouling process presented in the companion book *Lao Tzu's Tao Te Ching. Soul Journeying Commentaries. A Sojourning Pilgrim's Rendering of 81 Spirit Soul Passages.* Soul journeying and the enSouling process basically involve transforming and transitioning from being mostly unconsciously ego-identified with the world, others, ego, mind and body to being mostly consciously Soul-identified with the Multiverse, Beings, Self, Psyche and Spirit.

Disidentifying from the ego/personality in Assagioli's Psychosynthesis opens the way to Soulfully identifying *as* a Deeper/Higher Self. Individuating from collective ego-complexes/persona in Jung's Analytic Psychology opens the way to identifying *as* an *animus/anima* Soul and Archetypal Self. Spiritually awakening from the Soul-sickness of deficient ego-based to Meta/Being-centered needs/cognitions/values/motivations/love in Maslow's Self-ActualizationPsychology opens the way to 'Taoistic' receptivity/objectivity/helping and a Sacralized Self.

FAN

返

Revert
Return
Come back

HUI

回

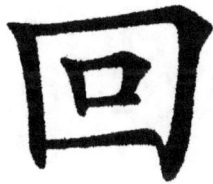

Revert to
Return to/from
Turn around/circle

KUEI

歸

Revert/return
To where one belongs
Converge/come together
Belong to/under care of

HSIANG

鄉

One's native place
Countryside
Village/hamlet
Hometown

RETURNING HOME TO THE REALITY/ ACTUALITY OF TAO AND OUR INNATE/ INHERENT/INTRINSIC TAO-NATURE

Appendix One
Quick Reference to the Narratives

The following is a quick reference to succinctly stated essential messages of/for each of the one-hundred eleven narratives of this rendition of *The Lieh Tzu* text.

Section One
The Nature of Originating/Heaven's Bestowal

1. Unborn/limitless/undifferentiated Wu Chi/Mysterious Female originate everything.
2. Cosmogonic sequencing of Wu Chi/primordial Ch'i/Yin-Yang/Heaven-Earth/all things.
3. Heaven covers/Earth supports/Yin-Yang interacting generates/sages inspire/teach.
4. Gain-loss/life-death/ other bipolarities are equal parts of the natural cycle of things.
5. Let the originating/returning and the uniting/dissolving of energy/things come/go.
6. Accepting the changes of life cycling through stages of infancy/youth/old age/death.
7. Happiness is living and dying is a liberating homecoming/returning to original nature.
8. Non-attaching to recognition through the emptiness/stillness of non-having/doing.
9. Not accelerating growing/delaying decaying/be accepting of their natural balancing.
10. The permanence of the vapor of Heaven/matter of Earth cannot really be counted on.
11. Our life/body/mind/Spirit are gifts on loan from Heaven-Earth beyond owning/control.

Section Two
The Nature of Transcending/Yellow Emperor

12. Enlightenment can involve not consciously thinking about

regulating/cultivating self.

13. Drifting/riding on the wind beyond distinctions/dualities/ barriers of ordinary ego-mind.
14. Gather energy/forget self/focus Spirit/transcend externals/ become one with Origin.
15. The art of living is being in a constant state of mind unaffected by any/all circumstances.
16. Experiencing the power of believing/not doubting/fearing and being able to accomplish.
17. Understanding/balancing/not going against the natural instincts of individual beings.
18. Understanding the being/nature/existence of things calmly without self-consciousness.
19. Trust/go with/not fight against what is meant to be in the natural course/flow of living.
20. Being in a state of non-knowing/merging with externals and being able to avoid harm.
21. Being able to exercise control over energy in the three elixir fields of the human body.
22. Non-attachment to displaying talents/becoming important and attracting a following.
23. Not regarding oneself as being enlightened and unable to befriend others in the world.
24. Being true to oneself/living beyond dualistic judgments based on external appearances.
25. The adaptive and survival value of being soft/flexible/yielding/flowing in living life.

Section Three

The Nature of Transforming/King Mu

26. Spirit-journeying beyond space-time and the interchangeability of reality and dreaming.
27. Birthing/dying are illusions based upon the uniting/dissolving of Yin/Yang Ch'i energy.
28. The rising/falling of Ch'i energies in our bodies follow the Ch'i energies of Heaven-Earth.

29. Dream life compensates/balances the circumstantial happiness/miseries of waking life.
30. Dreaming can be experienced as real and reality can be experienced as dreaming.
31. Having/losing memory can affect experiencing peacefulness/happiness/freedom.
32. Confusion/certainty about what is real/true/good/right is a matter of perspective.
33. Attaching to mental beliefs/emotional feelings about what is real can be deceptive.

Section Four
The Nature of Awakening/Confucius

34. Real happiness/true contentment involve letting go of ideas of happiness/contentment.
35. Harmonizing of body with mind/mind with energy/energy with Spirit/Spirit with living.
36. Possible sagehood involves being a real/true/honest/openhearted/trustworthy human.
37. Real wisdom involves recognizing strengths/weaknesses in ourselves/other human beings.
38. Still body/empty mind transcend external attractions/distractions of sensory experience.
39. Real traveling is the inner forgetting of/merging with externals with one's whole self.
40. Real enlightenment is accepting its naturalness and not considering it to be strange.
41. Celebrating a fulfilling life and lamenting an untimely death are naturally appropriate.
42. Enlightened human beings equally accept the natural course of both living and dying.
43. Being a skilled practitioner may not go along with being an effective administrator.
44. Real strength may involve not encountering difficult situations necessitating its use.
45. Paradoxes can awaken human beings from the ignorance of

conventional knowings.

46. Withdrawing when work is finished is according with the natural way/order of Heaven.

SECTION FIVE

THE NATURE OF UNITING/T'ANG'S QUESTIONS

47. Things continually come/go and it is hard to ascertain beginnings/endings/boundaries.
48. Projects gradually progress/complete with patience/determination/Heavenly support.
49. Not priding in abilities/pushing beyond limits/competing with everything to the death.
50. Understanding the natural way of things/knowing and taking one's place in the universe.
51. Customs differ in different places and are only judged as being strange by outsiders.
52. Arguments over differences in the nature of inexlicable phenomena are meaningless.
53. Focusing/concentrating/balancing tension between push and pull/using a light touch.
54. Trying to integrate head and heart by exchanging one for the other creates problems.
55. Practicing involves mastering technique and developing a nondual heart connection.
56. Mastering an art involves a life-long commitment in order for it to be world-changing.
57. Kindred spirits are empathically attuned human beings /free of barriers between them.
58. There is no difference between real and artificial when both are regarded as natural.
59. Extensive training/practicing develop proficiency that can even make friends of rivals.
60. Training the body to obey mental commands involves a relaxed body and a clear mind.
61. Revenge that is handled without killing does not perpetuate a cycle of retaliatory killing.

Section Six
The Nature of Following/Destiny

62. Allow events to naturally unfold without attempting to promote success/prevent failure.
63. Fortunate or unfortunate lives do not reflect the worthiness or unworthiness of human beings.
64. Friends support greater abilities in each other in terms of what is best for a greater good.
65. The timeliness of living/dying involves the convergence of many uncontrollable factors.
66. Overvaluing/overattaching to the natural course of health/life can risk the loss of both.
67. The life course is determined more by the natural unfolding of events than by effort.
68. Honestly accepting the individual differences of people is better than feigning interest.
69. Many things happen without active intervention/accept outcomes with equanimity.
70. Nothing lasts forever/do not attach to either the desire for living or the fear of dying.
71. Valuing/appreciating/enjoying the precious gift of human life beyond its gain or its loss.

Section Seven
The Nature of Enjoying/Yang Chu

72. Not sacrifice integrity/honesty/humility pursuing empty rank/power/reputation/wealth.
73. Not lose heart by striving for/pursuing/attaining social recognition/gainful achievement.
74. Human life is short/transient/beyond control/make the best use of it and enjoy it.
75. Avoid both extremes of being either too poor or too rich and live with sufficient means.
76. Cultivating living is taking care of/not denying oneself/living simply/freely/contentedly.
77. Follow one's heart/not be constrained by social convention/

enjoy oneself/give freely.

78. Unrestricted pleasure and obsessive hard work both damage one's body/health/life.
79. Living/dying come by themselves/have their own natural course beyond one's control.
80. Let things alone/go their natural course without risking sacrificing one's bodily integrity.
81. Ruling is best done by gently encouraging from behind rather than leading from ahead.
82. Life is short/ impermanent/let it run its natural course and make the best use of it.
83. See through the illusions/worries of status/fame/wealth/longevity and live freely.

SECTION EIGHT

THE NATURE OF COMPLETING/SYNCHRONICITY

84. Actions produce reactions/causes produce effects like shadows/echoes follow light/sound.
85. Animal-like seeking/pursuing/grabbing for/clinging to wealth/power result in downfall.
86. Understanding the principles of consciously learning/accurately performing for success.
87. Effective leadership involves delegating responsibilities to mature/stable people.
88. One cannot imitate/compete with the naturally beautiful works/creations of Nature.
89. Not relying upon others' opinions of one's worth/value that can endanger oneself.
90. Success/good fortune may be a matter of being in the right place at the right time.
91. One is 'done to' by others for what one 'does to' others in form/kind/degree/extent.
92. Problems are solved by addressing/removing the causes rather than the symptoms.
93. Successfully navigating living involves trusting the situation and being self-confident.

94. The best way to keep/not reveal a secret about a planned action is by not acting on it.
95. Short-range achievements do not necessaily guarantee long-term accomplishments.
96. What initially appears to be bad fortune can later result in good fortune and vice versa.
97. Good/bad luck play significant determining roles in fortunate/unfortunate outcomes.
98. Seeing essences/potentials is seeing beyond the outer forms/appearances of beings.
99. Being a good/effective leader correlate with how well one is managing one's life.
100. Rank/ability/wealth are sources of envy/hatred/resentment and trouble in living.
101. One principle/practice does not always apply to all situations/at all times/in all places.
102. Sometimes retribution can be accidently triggered by circumstantial coincidences.
103. Not be so self-righteously judgmental that the necessary assistance of others is refused.
104. Dying for someone who values one and not dying for someone who does not is natural.
105. Learning is best accomplished by focusing on one method rather than many alternatives.
106. Natural reactions/behavior need to be understood and not misunderstood/punished.
107. Some know theories but cannot apply them and others apply them without knowing.
108. Real compassion for life is sparing it rather than celebrating it through sacrificing it.
109. Things/beings are not created exclusively for the benefit of other things/beings.
110. Shameful activities/wealth/opinions/guilt depend upon how one perceives them.
111. Preoccupations/obsessions result in ignoring surrounding realities and create danger.

Appendix Two
Quick Reference to Practical Guidelines

The following is a quick reference to essential practical guidelines for conducting the attending relationship/process with human beings as found in each of the one-hundred eleven narratives and/or commentaries of this rendition of *The Lieh Tzu* text.

Section One
The Nature of Originating/Heaven's Bestowal

1. Appreciating mysterious originating/assisting unique individualizing/natural unfolding.
2. Experiencing interconnectedness/alternating dynamics of Yin/Yang Ch'i vital energies.
3. Assisting actualizing equally worthwhile places to be/parts to play in the world/universe.
4. Accepting the transiency of living with equanimity/seeing through illusions of living/dying.
5. Aware that beginnings/endings are separations/joinings of primordial and Yin/Yang Ch'i.
6. Following the transforming of vital Ch'i energy through stages of infancy/youth/maturity.
7. Appreciating the completing of living as a happy homecoming to original/true Tao-nature.
8. Not investing in/attaching to/preferring of agendas/ strategies/techniques/outcomes.
9. Allowing natural changes without trying to cause/control/ direct/manipulate/force them.
10. Not wastng time/energy on matters/issues/events beyond the power to control them.
11. Experiencing that living is a blessed gift/precious opportunity on loan from Heaven-Earth.

Section Two
The Nature of Transcending/Yellow Emperor

12. Modeling of a middle way between extremes of sensual indulgence/stressful overworking.
13. Experiencing that transcending the limitations of ego-mind involves extensive training.
14. Identifying with/*as* Original Tao/compounding Ch'i energy/uniting with the natural order.
15. Mastering conducting the attending relationship/process calmly under any/all conditions.
16. Fulfilling a deeply committed calling rather than accumulating any wealth in practicing.
17. Intuitive/empathic attuning to/according with/following of unique/individual Tao-natures.
18. Ease in naturally understanding/gracefully flowing with human nature/being/existence.
19. Following the natural fluctuating course of human living without resisting or fighting it.
20. Harmonizing/merging by being in a nondual/integral/empty state of pure consciousness.
21. Not publically displaying/commercially marketing extraordinary psychic powers/abilities.
22. Disinterested in creating/developing/maintaining a thriving practice of deferent followers.
23. Respect/warmth/availability/appropriateness in conducting the relationship/process.
24. Being beyond selectivity/value judgments based upon external appearances/behaviors.
25. Softness/flexibility/yielding/flowing dissolve defenses/resistances/power struggles.

Section Three
The Nature of Transforming/King Mu

26. No real phenomenological difference between the experiences of waking/dreaming life.
27. Transient transformative changes are the alternating/

reversing of bipolar Yin/Yang Ch'i.
28. Assisting understanding the correlations/compensations of waking and dreaming lives.
29. Experiencing in dream life can facilitate making corresponding changes in waking life.
30. Dreams can be experienced as real reality and real reality can be experienced as a dream.
31. Integrative value of remembering/reflecting upon/re-experiencing/reworking past events.
32. Conventional conceptions of clarity/good/right/well may be confused/bad/wrong/ill.

Section Four
The Nature of Awakening/Confucius
33. Therapeutic role-playing/re-enactments can activate the processing of emotional feelings.
34. Letting go of ideas of happiness opens the way to experiencing real/true happiness.
35. Instinctively/intuitively harmonizing/integrating body/mind /energy/Spirit/surroundings.
36. Open-hearted/natural/spontaneous/harmonious/smooth/realistic/trustworthy practicing.
37. Integrating both positive/negative and strong/weak characteristics/traits/qualities.
38. Cultivating non-knowing/having/doing/being and clearness/emptiness/stillness/freeness.
39. Objectifying external phenomena versus subjectfying internal states of consciousness.
40. Socially conditioned/conventionally/consensually accepted 'normality' may not be so.
41. Non-attaching to fixed/constant/conventional ways of responding to similar situations.
42. Accepting the transient natural life cycle and equally embracing both living and dying.
43. Difference of proficient/competent practicing and efficient/effective administrating.

44. Not displaying psychic/transformative/healing powers that accompany development.
45. Using paradox to awaken habitual/limiting conceptual ways of thinking/understanding.
46. Stepping back/allowing process to naturally unfold/proceed/develop/complete.

SECTION FIVE

THE NATURE OF UNITING/T'ANG'S QUESTIONS

47. Difficulty of ascertaining beginnings/endings of things and the boundaries between them.
48. Synchronistic/synergistic workings of Heaven-Earth to unblock obstacles to progressing.
49. Humbly/modestly working within the normal limits of mental/emotional capabilities.
50. Connecting with ordinary experiencing/everyday living and utopian visioning/idealizing.
51. All human beings are incomparably unique/different individually/culturally/normatively.
52. Real/true/natural intelligence/insight/intuition as opposed to learnedness/erudition.
53. Undistracted/undisturbed/focus/concentration on conducting the relationship/process.
54. Understanding unique constitution/character traits/personality qualities/behaviors.
55. Both technical proficiency/competency in skills/abilities and open/wholeheartedness.
56. Mastery of abilities in conducting the attending relationship/process is not completed.
57. Uniquely individual differences are bridged through active listening/empathic attuning.
58. What is unreal/artificial/crafted can effect real awakenings/changes/transformations.
59. Freedom from envying/competing with/trying to outdo teachers/students/therapists.
60. Conducting the attending relationship/process with a

relaxed body and still/clear mind.

61. Working out anger/grief/revenge through role-playing and prevent cycles of violence.

SECTION SIX

THE NATURE OF FOLLOWING/DESTINY

62. Successful/fortunate outcomes may be largely due to factors beyond conscious control.
63. Successful practice/professional reputation/fortunate outcome may be a matter of luck.
64. No personal investment in meeting own needs in the attending relationship/process.
65. Conflicting with human beings often results in empathic failures/derailed process.
66. May be unnecessary to 'treat' apparent 'illness' which is a matter of the natural life cycle.
67. Accepting the natural course/unfolding of living and being true to/trusting in oneself.
68. Offering feedback relevantly/concretely/directly/honestly without judging/feigning.
69. Not anticipating/calculating/predicting the probability of successful results/outcomes.
70. Using concerns/anxieties/fears/sadness about dying as catalysts for living more fully.
71. Appreciating/enjoying present living as a blessed gift/precious treasure/great opportunity.

SECTION SEVEN

THE NATURE OF ENJOYING/YANG CHU

72. Not sacrificing personal/professional integrity for wealth/status/reputation/power.
73. Being economical/efficient and not wasting precious lifetime on trivia/irrelevancies.
74. Realizing the transiency of human living and fully enjoying /making optimal use of it.
75. Accepting a sufficient personal/professional life without

toiling to 'make' a living.

76. Cultivating living contentedly/undetermined by the needs/wishes/demands of others.
77. Ignoring/transcending consensus realities may appear to be insane or enlightened.
78. Not denying/repressing instinctual nature/depleting vital energy through overworking.
79. Comfortably/peacefully accepting the life cycle without trying to increase the lifespan.
80. Valuing/harmonizing/sustaining the natural integrity/health of the physical body.
81. Guiding from behind rather than leading from ahead and possibly blocking progressing.
82. Understanding the impermanence of human living and not squandering vital energies.
83. Not fearing other's evaluations/making too little money/being relatively unknown.

Section Eight

The Nature of Completing/Synchronicity

84. Actions cause corresponding effects/reactions like shadows/echoes follow light/sound.
85. Not expend vital energies by desiring/pursuing/acquiring/possessing/hoarding wealth.
86. Understand intrapsychic dynamics/interpersonal processes/transpersonal dimensions.
87. Physical stability/emotional maturity/personal goal-direction seem to result in success.
88. Being creative/original/without trying to imitate/compete with Heaven-Earth/Nature.
89. Maintaining personal/professional boundaries by not requiring praise/accepting gifts.
90. Appreciating that successes may not be due to skills but rather to synchronicity/timing.
91. Contentment with 'caseload' size without tapping referral sources of other colleagues.

92. Working with deeper/underlying causes rather than treating presenting symptoms.
93. Trusting in the supporting structure/boundaries/limits of the relationship/process.
94. Not acting out evoked personal associations and working with them in own therapy.
95. Experiencing major successes with equanimity and not proudly or over-confidently.
96. Not making hasty assessments of/having fixed opinions about early successes/failures.
97. The same successful theories/techniques may be unsuccessful in different situations.
98. Intuitive awareness of essential nature/inherent potentials rather than appearances.
99. The parallels/correspondences between conducting personal life/professional practice.
100. Not experiencing the difficulties/stresses associated with striving for wealth/fame.
101. No one strategy/technique is guaranteed to result in success in similar situations.
102. Not acting out any intense/upsetting feelings occurring in the relationship/process.
103. Accepting assistance from others without judgmentally/self-righteously refusing it.
104. Abiding by professional ethics when experiencing transference/countertransference.
105. Not overwhelming human beings with too many options/alternatives/choices/paths.
106. Transcending mutually exclusive/either-or/dualistic differences in experiencing.
107. Understanding/integrating theoretical understanding/methodological practicing.
108. Compassionate honoring of human living without performing ritual observances.
109. Not prioritizing human being over that of other sentient beings through reciprocity.

110. Not suspecting motives/judging others/doubting reality based upon appearances.
111. Not so preoccupied with plans/strategies/outcomes that reality is not clearly seen.

Appendix Three
Summary of Four Experiential Concepts

The following succinctly summarizes the four principal experiential concepts of Te, Yin/Yang Ch'i, Wu Wei Ch'i and Tao and their modalities, Non-Being/Wu states, Being/Yu states and characteristics, qualities and activities.

Concept — *Te*

Unique individuality/potent Virtuosity.

Modality

Knowing/noetics/epistemology/'logic'/Truth/integrity/ wisdom.

Wu State

Non-knowing/Tao-'knowing'/non-mental 'contents'.

Yu State

Letting-be/clearness/clarity/lucidity/transparency.
Groundedness in the Clear Mirror of the Mind of Light.

Characteristics/qualities/activities---

Awareness/acknowledging/accepting/appreciating.
Non-altering/non-abstracting/non-assuming/non-attributing.
Concretizing/comprehending/non-construing/non-concluding.
Regarding/respecting/receiving/realizing.
Non-rejecting/non-revising/non-reforming/non-rationalizing.
Sanity/sentience/sensibility/sagacity.
Awakeness/alertness/attention/constant presence.

Concept — *Yin/Yang Ch'i*

Dynamic bipolarity/interdependent complementarity.

Modality

Having/dynamics/aesthetics/axiology/Good/beauty/harmony.

Wu State

Non-having/Tao 'having'/non-emotional 'goods'.

YU STATE

Letting-go/emptiness/vacuity/vacancy/voidness.
Centeredness in the Empty Vessel of the Heart of Love.

CHARACTERISTICS/QUALITIES/ACTIVITIES

Alternating/aligning/attuning/according.
Non-appropriating/non-acquiring/non-attaching/non-accumulating.
Counterbalancing/compensating/non-comparing/non-conflicting.
Relinquishing/releasing/reciprocating/reversing.
Non-refracting/non-rating/non-ranking/non-retaining.
Surrendering/simplicity/sufficiency/satisfaction.
Changing/transforming/empathy/continual balancing.

CONCEPT — *Wu Wei Ch'i*

Kinetic fluidity/Tao-sourced activity.

MODALITY

Doing/kinetics/ethics/politics/Right/grace/peace.

WU STATE

Non-doing/Tao-'doing'/non-volitional 'deeds'.

YU STATE

Going-with/stillness/tranquility/equanimity/calm.
Flowingness from the Still Point of the Will of Law.

CHARACTERISTICS/QUALITIES/ACTIVITIES

Allowing/acceding/agreeing/accompanying.
Non-administrating/non-attaining/non-achieving/non-accomplishing.
Complying/cooperating/non-controlling/non-coercing.
Resonating/responding/replying/returning
Non-regimenting/resisting/reacting/rebelling.
Sourcing/support/synergy/serenity.
Flowing/following/entraining/continuous unfolding.

CONCEPT — *Tao*

Ultimate Reality/intimate actuality.

MODALITY

Doing/ontics/ontology/metaphysics/Reality/unity/identity.

WU STATE

Non-Being/non-relational 'others'.

YU STATE

Being-with/oneness/unity/co-existing/intimacy.
Spaciousness as the Open Circle of the Spirit of Life.

CHARACTERISTICS/QUALITIES/ACTIVITIES

Associating/affiliating/allying/abiding.
Non-alienating/non-abandoning/non-abolishing/non-annihilating.
Connecting/communing/non-constricting/non-constraining.
Rejoining/reconnecting/reuniting/residing.
Non-restricting/non-restraining/non-reducing/non-repressing.
Symbiosis/Sacredness/splendor/Spirituality.
Concluding/completing/consummating/culminating wholeness.

APPENDIX FOUR
EXCERPTS FROM *THE WEN TZU*

The following are distilled, condensed and paraphrased excerpts from Cleary's translation of the text of *The Wen Tzu/ True Scripture of Understanding the Mysteries/T'ung Hsuan Chen Ching. The Wen Tzu* text is set in the Warring States/Chan Kuo period (c. 475-221 BCE) of the Eastern/Later Chou dynasty (c. 770-221 BCE); is later compiled by a disciple or circle of disciples of Lao Tzu and consists of further sayings, understandings and applications of Lao Tzu's wisdom.

The applications of *The Wen Tzu* text are observations and advisings for rulers spoken in the voice of Lao Tzu that 1) focus on the characteristics, attributes, qualities and activities of wise and unwise, true and untrue and real and unreal human beings in leadership positions, 2) detail the progressive decline, disintegration, degeneration, deterioration and devolution of society and humankind when they lose the original and natural unity, purity, vitality, simplicity and spontaneity of Spirit/Tao and 3) describe ways of being, living and statecraft that restore the real nature, dignity, equality and security of human beings; the true qualities, humanity, justice and fairness of leaders and the pure harmony, goodness, wholeness and freedom of society.

Interested readers are encouraged to study Cleary's introduction to, and translation of, *The Wen Tzu* text to experience and appreciate the depth, breadth and relevance of its applications to/for the psychological, psychosocial and socio-political realities and issues of our contemporary human being and living and their regulating and transforming and developing and evolving. The excerpts are included as an appendix to this rendition because of their sharing and amplifying a similar focus, Spirit and way of real human being as those of *The Lieh Tzu* text and for their relevant applications to ways of conducting and engaging and participating in the attending relationship/process of psychotherapy/counseling.

Lao Tzu says that Real Human Beings are:

1. Identifying *as* dark/deep/empty/still Tao that illuminates/births/fulfills/moves everything.
2. Being Tao-like and facilitating/guiding the unique inner Tao-nature/living of everything.
3. Acting in accord with how human beings are and the way in which life events unfold.
4. Embodying Heavenly Tao's purity/clarity/emptiness/ harmony/yielding/simplicity.
5. Being upright/straightforward/concentrated/unified/ open/clear/calm/wise/inSpirited.
6. Celestial/serving living/adapting to changes/inwardly centering/evolving with things.
7. Continually returning to the original/essential/unified inner Tao-nature of human beings.
8. Inwardly merging with the Spiritual light of Tao and the power of its water-like softness.
9. Being the humble/open/flexible/responsive/yielding/ following qualities of the feminine.
10. Formlessly not being calculating/clever/cunning/ contriving/devising/naming/defining.
11. Harmonizing Yin/Yang Ch'i energies and openheartedly connecting with Spirit/Tao.
12. Joining/emulating the Sacred/miraculous blessings/ celestial influences of Heavenly Tao.
13. Remaining connected with the Source/Tao in pure sincerity/impartiality/sufficiency.
14. Being like clear mirrors; seeking nothing /receiving/ reflecting everything/retaining nothing.
15. Not displaying achievements/accomplishments/name/ fame/Virtuosity/potency/efficacy.
16. Being humane/generous/dutiful/virtuous/inspiring/

nourishing/fostering/preserving.

17. Serving/cultivating/integrating/embodying vitality/ Spirit without indulging/displaying.
18. Freely wandering/in No-thingness/emptiness beyond external worldly conventions.
19. Naturally nourishing human beings with gracefulness/ without unfairness/commanding.
20. Regulating their bodies by not wasting vital Spiritual energy inwardly or outwardly.
21. Bringing about events naturally/spontaneously/ vitally/Spiritually/silently/sincerely.
22. Embracing reality/enacting sincerity/Spiritually influencing without commanding.
23. Identifying *as* the subtlety/spontaneity/unity of Mother Tao without possessing.
24. Enacting the unity/Virtuosity of Tao by assisting/ benefiting truthfully/happily/silently.
25. Faithfully rooted in Spiritual reality and are influencing without words/directives.
26. Inner-connected/motivated/directed and valued/ respected/enjoyed by human beings.
27. Truthful/harmonious/effect necessary/appropriate/ cooperative actions in human beings.
28. In touch with the source/foundation of Tao without cleverness/craftiness/talent/skill.
29. Constantly remembering/enacting far-reaching desires to assist/benefit human beings.
30. Being creative by not contriving/by intentional non-doing/by not using Spirit causally.
31. Appropriately accepting their place/economically according with their time in the world.
32. Regarding the world/its myriad things as light/slight and are not burdened/confused.

33. Not desiring/persuing/acquiring/accumulating status/rank/power/gain/profit/wealth.
34. Cultivating Tao/nourishing/harmonizing by Virtuosity/enjoying simplicity/sufficiency.
35. Embodying the clearness/evenness/stillness/freeness of Spirit/Heart-Mind naturally.
36. Attuning to/according with their unique nature/life conditions without desire/excess.
37. Nourishing their life through emptiness/stillness/light-heartedness/selflessness.
38. According with the natural laws of Tao's operations via clearness/emptiness/stillness.
39. Identifying with human beings/not coercing actions/not depleting vital Ch'i energies.
40. Reducing fullness/reversing completeness/accomplishing without striving/clinging.
41. Spontaneously enjoying themselves through non-attachment/inner experiencing/Spirit.
42. Quintessentially uniting withTao/internally regulating/clearly/Spiritually understanding.
43. Being Tao-like/with no depth-height/inside-outside/thinking-feeling/waking-dreaming.
44. Not abandoning Tao by taking private/arbitrary/motivated/worthy/unreasonable actions.
45. Harmoniously/peacefully/beneficially not devising/implementing/executing actions.
46. Safely/endlessly identifying *as* the encompassing canopy of Heaven/basic vehicle of Earth.
47. Not grasping-losing/contriving-failing/competing-exhausting/struggling-endangering.
48. Speaking the inexhaustibility of a single word and two/three/four words for the world.
49. Naturally passing away by not being careless/

immoderate/greedy/ambitious/invasive.

50. Enjoying the rewards/benefits of generosity/not the calamities/bitterness of greediness.
51. Discovering their destiny/regulating minds/ordering preferences/suiting their natures.
52. Cultivating their Virtuosity/enacting activity without expecting praise/resenting blame.
53. Preserving what they have/not seeking what they do not have/letting things come/go.
54. Not seeking/praise/reputation/fame for their knowledge/ability/accomplishments.
55. Not attached to/engaged in activities out of an over concern with self/fairness/honesty.
56. Being humble/non-demanding/cultivating their Virtuosity/uniting above and below.
57. Experiencing the sanity of inwardly accessing Essence/outwardly according with Reason.
58. Regulating body/harmonizng emotions/nourishing Spirit/living moderately/simply.
59. Following the naturalness/normality/neutrality/impartiality/sufficiency of the universe.
60. Not looking/acting strangely/abnormally/inappropriately/demonstrably/pretentiously.
61. According with destiny/not striving to make things come/prevent them from going.
62. Serenely/enjoyably taking pleasure in Tao and their inner Tao-nature/Virtuosity.
63. Not envying high status/hating important offices/resenting large incomes of others.
64. Avoiding the blindness/deafness of not seeing/hearing Tao by inquiring/listening.
65. Not desiring/seeking/pursuing/attaining good/justice/fame/reputation/profit/gain.

66. Experiencing that life is received from Heaven and outcomes occur through destiny.
67. Experiencing that Virtuosity/humility/value/respect/mastery begin with oneself.
68. Experiencing that the natural Way of Tao is losing by gaining/gaining by losing.
69. Having orderly minds/harmonious dispositions/realizing Tao/inner Tao-nature.
70. Experiencing that having power/treasures is not as good as finding/sourcing Tao.
71. Being at peace with themselves/flexible/yielding / meeting human beings as equals.
72. Listening sincerely/clearly/deeply/effectively by Spirit and not only with mind/ear.
73. Being immune to harm/injury by preventing intentions/fostering loving/assisting.
74. Nourishing/fostering/developing Virtuosity/unity/identity with Heaven-Earth/Tao.
75. Understanding that being their perfect Virtuosity is manifesting Tao's Heavenly design.
76. Experiencing that seeing/hearing are wisely knowing the root of fortune/misfortune.
77. Not intellectualizing/prognosticating/ingratiating/misunderstanding the Way of Tao.
78. Identifying *as* Tao's oneness/the foundation of Heaven-Earth/the unfolding of life.
79. Leading by holding to unity/not contriving activities/not capitalizing on Virtuosity.
80. Leading without pride/greed/anger/are responding for necessity/justice/rescuing.
81. Being successful by distrusting intelligence/neglecting calculation/not contriving results.
82. Being river-like/small of beginning/yielding/low of

flowing/following/of endless use.

83. Accepting of/adjusting/adapting/accomodating to/ according with the current times.
84. Guiding by Tao/nourishing with Virtuosity/holding to unity/living humbly/honestly.
85. Placing honesty/trustworthiness above emergent personal concerns/fixed behaviors.
86. Experiencing the mutual life-giving/nourishing/ respecting/loving presence of Tao.
87. Not letting present concerns/investments/attachments produce further concerns.
88. Leading by having no likes-dislikes/following natural laws and standard guidelines.
89. Not searching for truth in subjective judgments of right-wrong/pleasant-unpleasant.
90. Withdrawing when work is successfully accomplished/ not being arrogant/exhausted.
91. Utilizing the purity/Virtuosity of Tao to right wrongs/ order chaos/transform corruption.
92. Regulating the world's Heart into wellness/forgetting regulating the world's body.
93. Universally responding by embracing both complements of Yin/Yang Ch'i bipolarities.
94. Returning to the original Nonbeing of Tao by focusing inwardly on Yin/Yang Ch'i changes.
95. Experiencing the constant activity of Nature and its many Yin/Yang Ch'i compensations.
96. Identifying everything *as* oneself/harmoniously centering Yin/Yang Ch'i alternations.
97. Reaching Tao/embodying/personifying Virtuosity that is secretly/richly flowing within.
98. Integrating/utilizing the internal/external Yin/Yang Ch'i energies of formless Tao.

99. Understanding that real words/actions are spoken/acted without being spoken/acted.
100. Regulating behaviors/activities lawfully/appropriately/responsibly/meaningfully.
101. Experiencing Tao as a primordial stateless state that is powerfully transformative.
102. Understanding that intellectual knowing/trivial Virtuosity/false benevolence spoil Tao.
103. Experiencing that real/wise humanness is loving without resentments/punishments.
104. Experiencing that Virtuosity is developed by making weak strong/misfortune fortune.
105. Experiencing the essence of human being as clearness/harmony/stillness/joyfulness.
106. Seeing how things/matters/affairs are going and knowing how they will turn out.
107. Respecting the small/subtle, acting appropriately/timely, avoiding trouble/misfortune.
108. Minutely attentive/equally centered/inexhaustibly knowing/straightforwardly acting.
109. Observing the subtle origins of fortune/misfortune and seeing their conclusions.
110. Navigating changes in the wayfaring journey by understanding Nature/human nature.
111. Experiencing the reversings that beneficial things may be harmful and vice versa.
112. Being humanely/justly committed to ameliorating distress/benefiting human beings.
113. Rooted in wisdom/justice and flowing in depth/breadth that enrich human beings.
114. Loving nourishing human beings by nature and not for personal interests/use/gain.
115. Experiencing the mystery/infinity of Tao/Virtuosity

and of Yin/Yang Ch'i energies.

116. Heavenly/Earthly-like in their emptiness/equality/impartiality/equanimity/stillness.
117. Realizing the immensity/ultimacy/infinity/eternity of the silent/calm Spirit of Tao.
118. Experiencing that Tao/Heaven-Earth/Virtuosity are realized without invasion/coercion.
119. Covering like Heaven/supporting like Earth/harmonizing like Yin/Yang Ch'i energies.
120. Regarding all human beings as equally unique/valid/worthwhile/living suitable lives.
121. Living natural lives/adapting to circumstances/following human beings/human nature.
122. Not favoring/possessing/examining/misusing/punishing/executing human beings.
123. Making optimal/efficient/effective use of available resources/reasonable measures.
124. Allowing the natural flowing/unfolding of Wu Wei Ch'i energies without ambitions.
125. Unifying/working for humanity by assisting the weak/poor/needy/weary/elderly.
126. Progeny of Heaven regulating the world by means of the Heavenly Way of Tao.
127. Emulating Earthly-Heavenly Tao in stillness/following the sun/moon in actions.
128. Nourishing Spirit/Tao/the root of human living/regulating by nourishing in-fluence.
129. Understanding that successful regulating is rarely achieved by laws/punishments.
130. Taking living seriously/either conquering themselves or going along with their heart.
131. Being calm/uncontrived/suited to circumstances/following/preserving essential nature.

132. Knowing the true condition of life/destiny/not striving for life/worrying about destiny.
133. Not wishing to be wise/hating to be inferior and are avoiding conflict/contention.
134. Remembering the unity of Tao/detached from things/ returning to themselves.
135. Employing Spiritual illumination to regulate/ harmonize/settle the lives of human beings.
136. Characterized by purity/clarity/simplicity/harmony/ serenity/freedom/uniting with Tao.
137. Going along with customs/not acting independently of society/not opposing differences.
138. Being pure/simple/without artifice/complexity and are following the natural Way of Tao.
139. Being real human beings by closing the gateways of the senses and merging with Tao.
140. Being impartial/relying on Tao's balancing/according with the hearts of human beings.
141. Experiencing that non-doing is the allowing of/ according with the source/pattern of Tao.
142. Understanding Tao's absolute unity/according with alternating Yin/Yang Ch'i energies.
143. Succeeding by taking advantage of the times/ according with the wishes of human beings.
144. Cultivating their body by calm tranquility/nourishing their life by frugal economy.
145. Being stable/non-attached/fair/vast/empathically identifying with human beings.
146. Honoring living/valuing/caring for human beings/not injuring/burdening their body.
147. Nourishing/cultivating/regulating real Virtuosity in themselves and in human beings.
148. Being respectful/prudent/awestruck/cautious and

treating human beings well/fairly.

149. Not complicating affairs/not making demands that are difficult to manage/satisfy.

150. Leading by following/by avoiding favoritism/by Spiritual in-fluence/by not exploiting.

151. According with the seasons of Heavenly Tao above/ the patterns of Earthly Tao below.

152. Being compassionate toward human beings/partaking of the blessings of Heaven-Earth.

153. According with the interacting of Yin/Yang Ch'i energies and the balancing of bipolarities.

154. Experiencing that survival lies in cultivating/ practicing/attaining Tao/inner Tao-nature.

155. Practicing the goodness/rightness of Tao/not benevolence/righteousness/propriety.

156. Giving priority to the unitary roots of human being/ living not to its dualistic branchings.

157. According with/centering in/identifying *as* Tao and its natural spontaneity/Tzu Jan.

158. Enacting the impartiality of Tao by not desiring/ preferring/seeking/acquiring/possessing.

159. Leading by effectively benefiting human beings/ efficiently managing human affairs.

160. Not leading/regulating human beings via laws/rules/ regulations/directives/penalties.

161. Returning to simplicity/adapting/conforming to what is going on/not devising/contriving.

162. Being skillful at reinforcing/encouraging human beings with a minimal amount of effort.

163. Regulating in ways that are balancing what is large-small/light-heavy/vast-limited.

164. Being great in Virtuosity/greatly praiseworthy and not criticized for any minor failings.

165. Cultivating their Tao-nature/Virtuosity/not demanding perfection of human beings.
166. Not acting arbitrarily and are guiding by being humane/just toward human beings.
167. Bringing clarity/stability/safety to the confusions/disorders/dangers of human beings.
168. Happily living their lives uniquely/naturally/appropriately without useless activities.
169. Not opposing Heavenly Tao by being unfair/violent/cruel toward other human beings.
170. Being humane/just toward human beings and are winning the hearts of the wise/good.
171. Regarding human beings with the same honor/respect they have for parents/children.
172. Naturally returning to the ultimate/essential nonbeing/vastness of their Tao-nature.
173. Balancing/equalizing/harmonizing Yin/Yang Ch'i energies without using fixed policies.
174. Following the patterns/changes/transformings/cycles/reversings/returnings of Nature.
175. Understanding the root causes of what/why/how they are desiring/acting/enjoying.
176. Acting in accord with the pure simplicity/original harmony of their essential Tao-nature.
177. Complying with the natural harmonizing of Yin/Yang Ch'i dynamics/Wu Wei Ch'i kinetics.
178. Aligning with/attuning to/according with the fundamental harmonizing of Nature/Tao.
179. Not being imposing/intrusive/invasive/interfering in relation to other human beings.
180. Exerting a calming/harmonious/sufficient/restful influence upon other human beings.

SHEN	HSIN	SHEN
身	心	神
Body/trunk Self/person I/me/oneself The whole lifteime	Heart-mind Center/core Affections/feelings Intelligence/thinking Intentions/motives	Spirit/Spiritual Divinity/diety/god Supernatural energy Soul/Mind/genius

The Body-Spirit/Spirit-Body/Human Soul Centered Deep Within Our Human Heart

Sacred/wise/true/genuine/authentic/real Human Being is the harmonious integration of our human body and Spirit, *as* our Human Soul, centered deep within our Human Heart.

Our Human Soul is both an embodied Spirit and an inSpirited body, an incorporated body-Spirit and an animated Spirit-body. Throughout the time of our human life course, life cycle and lifespan, Spirit is descending and coalescing *as* our human body and body is ascending and evanescing *as* our Human Spirit. The awakened and conscious integration of our body and Spirit constitute our oneness, fullness, wholeness and completeness as a unique Human Being.

Being only a body without Spirit is being a despirited body suffering a sub/non-human life of horror as a dark compacted spasm of dried flesh longing for rain. Being only a Spirit without a body is being a disembodied Spirit suffering a sub/non-human life of terror as a dark gaping schism of gaseous vapor fearing the wind.

EPILOGUE ONE

A listing of words is provided for each of the four principal experiential concepts of Te, Yin/Yang Ch'i, Wu Wei Ch'i and Tao. Referred to as 'The Fours', the listed words are not bipolar complements or exact synonyms for each of the concepts but, rather, are close associations that add extended meaning to a general understanding of the ways of being and living toward which they point.[17]

TE —

Letting-be/Non-'knowing' of mental 'contents'.

Abstaining/non-attributing.
Beholding/non-believing.
Considering/non-concluding.
Describing/non-defining.
Exploring/non-explaining.
Fidelity/non-forecasting.
Genuineness/non-guessing.
Honesty/non-hypothesizing.
Interest/non-imputing.
Justice/non-justifying.
Keenness/non-knowing 'about'.
Luminosity/non-labeling.
Magnetism/non-misinterpreting.
Naturalness/non-naming.
Observing/non-opining.
Presence/non-presupposing.
Quintessence/non-questioning.
Realizing/non-reckoning.
Sagacity/non-speculating.
Trusting/non-testing.
Uprightness/non-upending.
Veracity/non-vulgarity.
Witnessing/non-worthlessness.

YIN/YANG CH'I —

Letting-go/Non-'having' of emotional 'goods'.

Adjusting/non-accumulating.
Balancing/non-biasing.
Complementing/non-clinging.
Divesting/non-displaying.
Equalizing/non-entangling.
Forgetting/non-favoring.
Generosity/non-grasping.
Harmonizing/non-hoarding.
Impartiality/non-investing.
Juxtaposing/non-judging.
Kindness/non-keeping.
Losing/non-lusting.
Mutuality/non-measuring.
Nirvana/non-needing.
Oscillating/non-owning.
Periodicity/non-preferring.
Quality/non-questing.
Regulating/non-retaining.
Surrendering/non-seizing.
Transiency/non-taking.
Unattaching/non-unilaterality.
Vacuity/non-vanity.
Withdrawing/non-wanting.

WU WEI CH'I —
Going-with/Non-'doing'
of volitional 'deeds'.

Approving/non-aggressing.
Benefiting/non-battling.
Complying/non-contending.
Developing/non-directing.
Endorsing/non-exploiting.
Following/non-forcing.
Guiding/non-goading.
Humility/non-hindering.
Inventing/non-interfering.
Journeying/non-jousting.
Knack/non-kowtowing.
Letting/non-legislating.
Malleability/non-manipulating.
Navigating/non-niggling.
Obeying/non-opposing.
Permitting/non-prodding.
Quieting/non-quarreling.
Relaxing/non-resisting.
Sanctioning/non-struggling.
Tranquility/non-tampering.
Unfolding/non-'using'.
Verifying/non-violating.
Wayfaring/non-warfaring.

TAO —
Being-with/Non-'being'
of relational 'others'.

Adjoining/non-abandoning.
Belonging/non-betraying.
Connecting/non-colluding.
Dwelling/non-dissociating.
Engaging/non-estranging.
Fulfilling/non-fragmenting.
Gathering/non-gaming.
Humanness/non-harming.
Including/non-isolating.
Joining/non-jesting.
Kindredness/non-keyholing.
Liberating/non-limiting.
Meeting/non-marginalizing.
Negotiating/non-neglecting.
Oneness/non-oppressing.
Partnering/non-patronizing.
Quickening/non-qualifying.
Remembering/non-reducing.
Sharing/non-stigmatizing.
Togetherness/non-targeting.
Uniting/non-unconnecting.
Validating/non-victimizing.
Warmness/non-'wronging'.

Epilogue Two

This concluding epilogue identifies, characterizes, summarizes and amplifies some of the essential focuses, characteristics, qualities and activities of the four principal experiential concepts of Te, Yin/Yang Ch'i, Wu Wei Ch'i and Tao that can provide a ground, center, flow and matrix from/by which to awaken and open a conscious way of human being and living and an attentive way of conducting the attending relationship/process of psychotherapy/counseling.

Te — *inborn Tao-nature/unique individuality/potent Virtuosity/Tao-sourced nature.*

upper/head/mental energy center/elixir field/conception/ cognitive/thinking.
noticing/beholding/witnessing/observing.
awakening/accepting/acknowledging/appreciating.
regarding/respecting/recognizing/receiving/revealing.
discerning/comprehending/understanding.
illuminating/enlightening/consciousness/awareness.
mental clearness/clarity/noetics/epistemology/'logic'.
Truth/integrity/wisdom.
human dignity/authenticity/efficacy/radiancy/ transparency.
character/excellence/trustworthiness.
trueness/kindness/humility/respecting being/living.
embodying of natural laws/order.

uniquely individualized nature/situation of psychotherapy/counseling.
ground/foundation/basis of psychotherapy/counseling.
psychotherapeutic presence/potency/co-creating/constantly.
questions to answer/what is true?
non-dualities of subject-object/knower-known/concepts/ objects.

clear mirror/receiving from a clear mind/not 'cloudy'/ 'crazy'/'dumb'.
ignorance-free of mental 'clutter', e.g., fantasies/beliefs/ opinions/'data'.
non-presupposing/preconceiving based upon similar 'issues'.
intrasubjectivity/non-rigid rules/recipes.
meditative concentrating/heart-mind fasting[18]/abstaining/ illumination.
awakenings/enlightenings/discoveries/revelations/epiphanies.
vitalistic/energetic/authentic individualizing.
Earth supports/grounded/solid/Mystery of originating[19]/ conception/Light.
awesomeness of real/actual human being/living.

YIN/YANG CH'I — *dynamic bipolarity/interdependent complementarity/Tao-sourced changes.*
middle/heart/emotional energy center/elixir field/ emotion/affective/feeling.
alternating/counterbalancing/compensating/centering.
adjusting/aligning/attuning/according.
reducing/relinquishing/reciprocating/reflecting/reversing.
interrelating/interacting/interchanging.
balancing/harmonizing/equalizing/voiding.
emotional emptiness/vacuity/dynamics/aesthetics/axiology.
Good/harmony/beauty.
human equality/impartiality/vacancy/mercy/transiency.
compassion/empathy/caring.
goodness/fairness/equity/valuing being/living.
according with natural changes/transformations.

dynamicaly shifting conditions/transformings of psychotherapy/counseling.
center/axis/pivot of psychotherapy/counseling.
psychotherapeutic polarity/parity/correlating/continually.
conflicts to resolve/what is 'good'?

non-dualities of either-or/this-that/judgments/objections.
empty vessel/reflecting from an empty heart/not 'sticky'/ 'ugly'/'bad'.
attachment-free of emotional 'baggage', e.g., desires/fame/ wealth/'power'.
non-associating/comparing based upon previous 'cases'.
interchangeability/non-rigid ratings/rankings.
meditative reflecting/sitting forgetting[18]/relinquishing/ intuition.
changes/transformations/fluctuations/alternations/reversals.
harmonic/syntonic/empathic attuning.
fire transforms/centered/mutable/Miracles of forming[19]/ gestation/Love.
amazement of real/actual human being/living.

WU WEI CH'I — *kinetic fluidity/yielding/complying/ following/Tao-sourced activity.*

lower/belly/volitional energy center/elixir field/conation/ conative/acting.
flexing/flowing/circulating/cycling.
allowing/acceding/assisting/accompanying.
resonating/replying/responding/revolving/returning.
flowing/coursing/streaming.
yielding/following/complying/conforming.
volitional stillness/tranquility/kinetics/ethics/politics.
Right/grace/peace.
human ability/flexibility/agency/fluency/efficiency.
frictionless/effortless/seamless.
rightness/softness/gentleness/serving being/living.
complying with natural course/unfolding.

kinetically unfolding processes/developing of psychotherapy/counseling.
flow/course/evolving of psychotherapy/counseling.
psychotherapeutic process/proceeding/collaborating/

continuously.
problems to solve/what is 'right'?
non-dualities of actor-action/doer-deeds/techniques/ objectives.
still point/responding from a still will/not 'busy'/ 'wrong'/ 'inept'.
error-free of volitional 'pulls', e.g., drives/impulses/habits/ 'feats'.
non-implementing/executing based upon previous 'tactics'.
interactive/non-rigid regimens/rituals.
meditative contemplating/Origin wandering[18]/instinct.
serving/encouraging/supporting/facilitating/guiding.
rhythmic/cyclic/synergic entraining.
water sustains/fluid/flowing/Marvels of manifesting[19]/ parturition/Law.
astonishment of real/actual human being/living.

TAO — *Ultimate Reality/intimate actuality/Tao-sourced identity.*
integrating of belly/heart/head energy centers/ integration/integrative/uniting.
co-existing/inter-being/unifying/synthesizing associating/affiliating/allying/abiding.
rejoining/reconnecting/reuniting/residing.
joining/connecting/communing.
fulfilling/completing/consummating/culminating.
relational oneness/unity/ontics/metaphysics/ontology.
Real/unity/identity.
human identity/universality/primacy/ultimacy/supremacy.
oneness/wholeness/liberty/sanctifying of being/living.
Sacredness/co-existing/interbeing.
Personifying of natural being/relationships.

integrally conjoining/intersubjectively completing of psychotherapy/counseling.

matrix/Selves/Beings/Souls Spirit of psychotherapy/ counseling.
psychotherapeutic partnering/participating/culminating/ completely.
separations to heal/what is 'real'?
non-dualities of self-other/whole-part/patients/ objectifications.
full circle/relating from a free Spirit/not 'messy'/ 'strange'/ 'alien'.
separation-free of relational 'others', e.g., egos/personas/ ciphers/ 'masks'.
non-stereotyping/profiling based upon previous 'appearances'.
intersubjectivity/non-rigid roles/regalia.
meditative absorption/Tao residing[18]/intimacy.
essences/universals/humanness/community/Sacredness.
organic/holistic/synchronic co-existing.
air surrounds/spacious/splendid/Magnificence of completing[19]/maturation/Life.
admiration of real/actual human being/living.

Te is a '*letting-be*' such that mental thinking/conceiving are grounded in an ignorance-free clarity/clearness of mind that opens a way to witnessing, acknowledging, accepting and appreciating unique individualities, excellence, Virtuosity and genius with dignity and respect and to experiencing discerning, comprehending and understanding what is True, authentic and wise without knowing a/any 'thing'. The clear mirror and high mountains of our Human Soul's Mind of Light.

Yin/Yang Ch'i is a '*letting-go*' such that emotional feeling/ desiring are centered in an attachment-free vacuity/emptiness of heart that opens a way to aligning with, attuning to, according with and alternating with changing bipolarities, transformings, compensations and reversals with equality and impartiality and to experiencing sufficiency, satisfaction and contentment with what is Good, harmonious and beautiful without having a/any 'thing'. The empty vessel and deep valleys of our Human Soul's Heart of Love.

Wu Wei Ch'i is a '*going-with*' such that volitional acting/doing are sourced in an error-free tranquility/stillness of will that opens a way to frictionlessly yielding to, effortlessly flowing with, seamlessly following and naturally accompanying circulatings, cyclings, revolvings and returnings with flexibility and facility and to experiencing supporting, affirming and guiding what is Right, graceful and peaceful without doing a/any 'thing'. The still point and flowing waters of our Human Soul's Will of Law.

Tao is a '*being-with*' such that relational existing/being are joined in a separation-free unity/oneness of Spirit that opens a way to associating, affiliating, allying and abiding with human Selves, Beings, Souls and Spirit with universality and identity and to experiencing fulfilling, consummating and culminating what is Real, whole and free without being a/any 'thing'. The open circle and vast skies of our Human Soul's Being of Life.

Concluding, completing, consummating and culminating experiences in, and the life of, the attending relationship/process of psychotherapy/counseling are the spontaneous presencings/Tzu Jan of the myriad diverse phenomena/Wan Wu occurring in/*as* the awakened consciousness and awarenesses of Tao-identifying real attenders/Shih Jen conducting, and of real human beings/Shih Jen engaging in, a real attending relationship/process.

Fulfilling the work of psychotherapy/counseling naturally opens the way to awakening, developing, progressing and evolving from being unconsciously and/or mostly exclusively identified with the illusionary life of an ego to transforming into being consciously and/or mostly inclusively identifying *as* Tao, Virtuosity/Te and the real being and living of a Human Soul and Spirit.[20]

Coda

Lieh Tzu's *Nature of Real Living/Hsing Shih Sheng* is the third volume of a *Taoist Trilogy* that includes Lao Tzu's *Tao Virtuosity Experience/Tao Te Ching* and Chuang Tzu's *Interior Records/Nei P'ien.* The narratives and commentaries of the *Nature of Real Living/Hsing Shih Sheng* depict the nature, qualities, attributes, activities and relationships of Real Human Beings/Shih Jen and of real attenders who are conducting the attending relationship/ process of psychotherapy/counseling; both of whom are embodying, personifyng, enacting and modeling a way of human being/ living that is identified with/*as* Tao and its dynamic-kinetic Yin/ Yang Ch'i and Wu Wei Ch'i operations and that is awakened, real, natural and practical.

Identifying with/*as* the Spirit, Heart and Soul of Lieh Tzu and with Real Human Beings/Shih Jen and real attenders, as characterized in the narratives and commentaries of the *Nature of Real Living/Hsing Shih Sheng*; opens the Way to ourselves being real human beings and real attenders who are attentively relating to human beings and who are being attentively related to by them. The Way is opened to being our own real Selves and to really living our own lives in heartfelt, wholehearted and heartwarming ways that are more awake, conscious, realistic, natural, intimate, practical, sustainable and fulfilling and that optimally and gratefully integrate our Heavenly Spirit and Earthly body *as* our Human Soul.

REFERENCES

The narratives in the following books were consulted, studied, cross-referenced, correlated, meditated on, edited, abridged, distilled, condensed, paraphrased and used for the preparation of this rendition.

Giles, Lionel (Trans.). *Taoist Teachings from the Book of Lieh Tzu.* Wisdom of the East. London: John Murray. 1912/1947. Cranmer-Byng, J. L. (Ed.). London: Forgotten Books. 2008.

Graham, A. C. (Trans.). *The Book of Lieh Tzu: A Classic of Tao.* New York: Columbia University Press. 1960. Morning Star Edition. 1990.

Wong, Eva (Trans.). *Lieh Tzu: A Taoist Guide to Practical Living.* Boston: Shambhala Publications, Inc.. 1995.

The following reference materials were consulted and used for all information concerning Chinese language, characters and etymologies and Taoist history, philosophy and terms in the preparation of this rendition.

Cleary, Thomas (Trans.). *The Taoist Classics: Vol. 1.* Boston: Shambhala Publications, Inc.. 1990.

Danian, Zhang. *Key Concepts in Chinese Philosophy.* Edmund Ryden (Ed. & Trans.). New Haven: Yale University Press/ Beijing Foreign Language Press. 2002.

Dong, Li. Concise *Chinese Dictionary: Chinese-English/English-Chinese.* Rutland, Vermont: Tuttle Publishing. 2015.

Fenn, C.H.. *The Five Thousand Dictionary: Chinese-English.* Cambridge: Harvard University Press. 1976.

Fischer-Schreiber, Ingrid. *The Shambhala Dictionary of Taoism.* Werner Wunsche (Trans.). Boston: Shambhala Publications, Inc.. 1996.

Huang, Quanyu; Chen, Tong and Huang, Kuangyan. *McGraw-Hill's Chinese Dictionary & Guide to 20,000 Essential*

Words. New York: McGraw Hill. 2010.

Kluemper, Michael L. and Nadeau, Kit-Yee Yam. *Mandarin Chinese Characters Made Easy*. Rutland, Vermont: Tuttle Publishing. 2016.

Matthews, Alison and Matthews, Laurence. *Learning Chinese Characters*. Rutland, Vermont: Tuttle Publishing. 2007.

Matthews, R.H.. *Matthew's Chinese-English Dictionary*. Cambridge: Harvard University Press. 1943.

McNaughton, William and Ying, Lee. R*eading and Writing Chinese: Traditional Character* Edition. Rutland, Vermont. Tuttle Publishing. 1999.

Wieger, L.. *Chinese Characters: Their Origin, Etymology, History, Classification and Signification*. L. Davrout (Trans.). New York: Dover Publications, Inc.. 1965.

Wilder, G.D. and Ingram, J.H.. *Analysis of Chinese Characters*. New York: Dover Publications, Inc.. 1974.

Wong, Eva. T*aoism: An Essential Guide*. Boston: Shambhala Publications, Inc.. 1997.

In the preparation of this rendition, all information concerning English language definitions was obtained from the following reference:

Webster's New Collegiate Dictionary. Springfield, Massachusetts: G. & C. Merriam Co.. 1979.

About the Author

Ray Vespe received his B.A. Psychology degree from Cornell University (1958), M.S. Clinical Psychology degree from Case Western Reserve University (1959) and Ph.D. Counseling Psychology degree from the California Institute of Integral Studies (1986). He has educated, trained, supervised, counseled and mentored graduate students in the Integral Counseling Psychology program at CIIS (1972-1990), the Transpersonal Psychology program at the California Institute of Transpersonal Psychology (1977-1979) and the Transpersonal Counseling Psychology program at John F. Kennedy University (1978-1990). Ray has worked in a wide variety of inpatient, outpatient, agency and group treatment settings and was Clinical Director of the Integral Counseling Center (1975-1978/1982-1990), San Leandro Community Counseling (1990-1992) and Marin Treatment Center (1992-2004). He has been a student of Tao for sixty-two years, has engaged in psychotherapy work for fifty-seven years and has maintained a licensed private practice for forty-four of those years. Ray is currently retired and living in Sonoma County, California.

www.ingramcontent.com/pod-product-compliance
Lightning Source LLC
Chambersburg PA
CBHW070054080526
44586CB00013B/1055